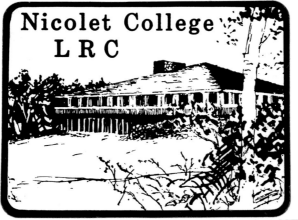

Hopi Cookery

Hopi Cookery

Juanita Tiger Kavena

THE UNIVERSITY OF ARIZONA PRESS
Tucson, Arizona

About the Author

JUANITA TIGER KAVENA applied for a teaching position on the Hopi Reservation in 1948 and "began an adventure that will last the rest of my life." Born into a Creek family, she was raised and educated in Oklahoma in Bureau of Indian Affairs and public schools, and at East Central State College. Later, as a home economist on the Hopi Reservation, she came into wide contact with the Hopi people and became interested in their native foods. She married a Hopi, Wilmer Kavena, and has been adopted into the Hopi tribe.

Fourth printing 1990

THE UNIVERSITY OF ARIZONA PRESS

Copyright © 1980
The Arizona Board of Regents
All Rights Reserved
Manufactured in the U.S.A.

Library of Congress Cataloging in Publication Data

Kavena, Juanita Tiger.
    Hopi cookery.

    Includes index.
    1. Hopi Indians — Food. 2. Indians of North
America — Southwest, New — Food. 3. Cookery, Indian
I. Title.
E99.H7K38   641.59′297   80-414

ISBN 0-8165-0618-3

This book is dedicated to all the wonderful Hopi women who, through their industriousness when food is at a premium, make Hopi family life a good life. May the Creator of all life bless them with good kind hearts and a rich productive life, especially my mother-in-law, Rena Kavena.

3-3-92

Contents

A Word From the Author

In the heart of many Indians is the desire to tell about "my people," to present them in such a way that others will understand their way of life, their place in the world, their contributions. Native foods and recipes are basic to the Hopi culture, and the many Hopi women with whom I worked over the years—true to their Indian desire to tell about their people—encouraged me to record as much as I could about their foods and methods of growing and preparing them. Many even invited me to their homes to taste special dishes they had prepared, hoping I would include the recipes in my book.

I began gathering information for this book as far back as the fifties, while I was working as a home extension agent on the Hopi Reservation. In the spring of 1948, a friend and I had applied for teaching positions on the reservation, and that summer we traveled over dirt roads from Holbrook, Arizona, northeast to the Hopi Agency in Keams Canyon. There were no farms or recognizable houses along the way, and we wondered where the people lived and what lay ahead for us.

At first I shared morning duties with a dormitory matron and taught home economics in the afternoon, including keeping the coal stove burning in the classroom. The children were responsive and would bring treats to share with me, such as cottonwood balls, parched cornmeal, dried fruit, and roots they had dug. Later, as a home economist with the Agricultural Extension Service, I worked with Indian women in such areas as meal planning, food preparation and preservation, and food storage. I visited many villages on both the Hopi and Navajo Reservations, tasting the various dishes that were offered to me and learning all I could about native foods.

Wherever man has lived, he has had to turn to his environment for a diet that would supply his vitamin and mineral needs. The Hopi people are no different. Through the method of trial and error, they, too, have learned to survive in their environment—albeit a parched and desolate area with seemingly little to offer for sustenance. Actually, more than two hundred plant species grow on the Hopi Reservation, many of which are used for food, medicine, and industry. I have been able to include only a small portion of Hopi foods in this book and, in fact, have only begun to touch on the early environmental foods that have disappeared from use with the advent of progress and packaged foods. However, these foods were vital in the development of our country and should not be forgotten. By sharing their knowledge of environmental foods with the early Anglo settlers, the Indians helped them to survive.

According to my homemakers, the Hopi way of life is dependent on each member's contribution to ensure harmony and peace, much as the strength of a chain is dependent on individual links. I hope this book will be a link that will inspire other Hopis to become more involved with their native foods and way of life—to preserve what is good in their culture, and learn to be selective with replacements.

Acknowledgments

I want to thank the following people for helping me, in ways too numerous to mention, to make this book possible: Edna Adams, Doris Calloway, Margaret Calnimptewa, Kenneth Carpenter, Betty Chaca, Ada Fredericks, June Gibbs, Stella Huma, Josephine James, Elda Joshongeva, Elsa Nashsonhoya, Gerald Stairs, and my mother-in-law, Rena Kavena, and the late Phyllis Adams.

Special thanks are due also to Marie Levy of Tucson, Arizona, for her thoughtful reflection on various aspects of Hopi culture. I also want to thank my family for their patience; Judith Randolph, secretary at the reservation's Home Extension Service, for typing and proofing the manuscript; and the University of Arizona Press for bringing about publication.

J.T.K.

Introduction

The ancestors of the Hopis were probably among the earliest people to live in the area which is now the southwestern United States. A myth regarding the origin of the Hopi way of life describes the wandering of these people as they searched for a Promised Land. According to tradition, this land was to provide them with wild game, soil suitable for their crops, a dependable water supply, and security from their enemies. Most of the wandering clans eventually settled on the mesas of the high plateau country east of the Little Colorado River in northern Arizona. By the time Coronado's men, the first Europeans to explore the Southwest, arrived in 1540, the Hopis were well established in their chosen area with a population exceeding ten thousand and a complex society that included religion, arts and crafts, multiple-dwelling housing, the practice of medicine, domesticated wildlife, and fields of cultivated cotton, corn, and other produce.

The Hopi reservation, which lies between the San Francisco Peaks and the Lukachukai Mountains, is spread out over First Mesa, Second Mesa, and Third Mesa in northeastern Arizona. Most Hopis live in villages on the mesas, but a few ranchers live in isolation far out on the plateaus. Hopi society is matrilineal and is based on the extended family, which is referred to as a clan. A typical family home is made up of three rooms—living room, kitchen, and sleeping area. Floors are of packed clay, at least in the older homes; they are sprinkled with water and polished with stones but still follow the rocky contours of the mesa tops.

The Hopis are peace-loving and center their lives on their centuries-old religion, which means morning and evening prayers and participation in many seasonal ceremonies. Despite their innate desire to be in harmony with their surroundings, life in the Promised Land has not always been tranquil. In addition to pestilence and famine brought on by drought, the Hopis were besieged by other

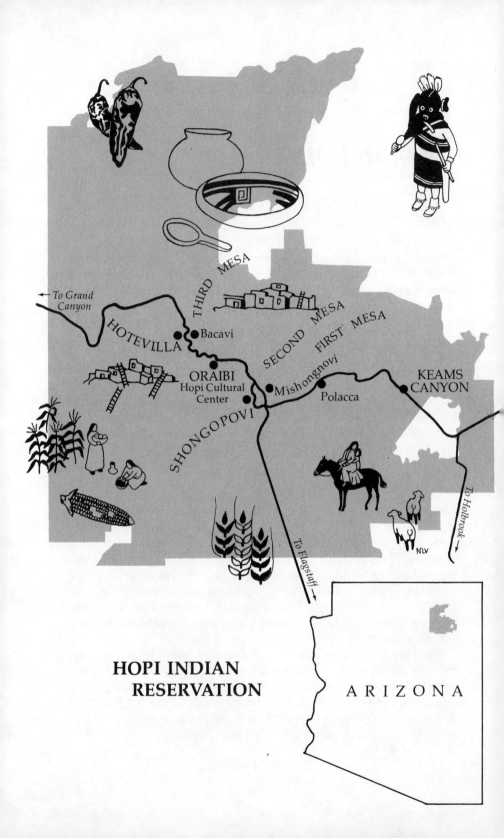

To Grand Canyon

THIRD MESA

SECOND MESA

FIRST MESA

HOTEVILLA

Bacavi

ORAIBI
Hopi Cultural Center

SHONGOPOVI

Mishongnovi

Polacca

KEAMS CANYON

To Holbrook

To Flagstaff

HOPI INDIAN RESERVATION

ARIZONA

Indian tribes that moved into the area—first the Utes, then the Apaches, and finally the Navajos who settled to the north of the Hopis. Nonetheless, the Hopis not only endured but fashioned a fruitful existence in a harsh environment.

Tradition versus Technology

Although basically an agrarian people—there is evidence that early Hopis grew melons, squash, beans, peas, and, later, various vegetables brought in by the Europeans, in addition to cotton and corn—the Hopis also hunted for food. Large game such as deer and elk stalked the nearby mountain ranges, and smaller rabbits, prairie dogs, quail, and doves were plentiful in the plateau region itself. Early housewives roasted the meat over open fires or in cooking pits, or made stews in big pottery pots.

The early kitchens had fireplaces for cooking (later, wood-burning stoves) and piki-making and stone-grinding areas. Most of the utensils were made of pottery, natural straws, or wood, and, besides the stew pot, included such essentials as bean pots, coffee pots, ladles, storage containers, and a long, hollow-handled dipper for getting water out of the springs. There were also grinding stones, piki-making stones, stone mortars and pestles, sturdy greasewood stirring sticks, gourd dippers, bundles of peach twigs and broom straws for straining liquids, piki trays, baskets for winnowing and sifting, and corn husks and leaves for wrapping foods and for using as cooking containers. Eating utensils consisted of pottery bowls for beans and stews, and gourd spoons. When there were not enough individual bowls to go around, the family shared a common bowl, a practice that is still followed when there are lots of guests.

Some of these items can still be found in the kitchens of older Hopis, but, by the 1970s, the pottery utensils had given way in most homes to more sturdy aluminum or stainless steel or even to pressure cookers, the grinding stones to electric grinders and the more efficient food mills. Many were also buying refrigerators, freezers, and electric stoves, and the fireplaces for making piki and culinary ashes were more often than not being set up in a special, small building outside.

Technology has also had an effect on the foods the Hopis eat. The ancestral Hopis based their diet on staples such as corn and beans, growing and preparing the foods themselves and producing remarkable harvests from their arid land. But, although there is still considerable farming and some cattle and sheepherding being done on the reservation, many Hopis drive seventy-five miles to the nearest Anglo supermarkets to buy the more convenient processed foods. For example, blue cornbreads are being replaced by tortillas made from all-purpose white flour. Powdered and canned milks are used routinely, rather than fresh milk.

Hopis like to entertain their friends, and serving food is a fundamental expression of Hopi hospitality. In fact, many a conflict has been averted by serving refreshments to the angry parties and giving them a chance to cool their tempers. Fruit and cornmeal drinks, Hopi tea, and corn tortillas are some of the traditional foods that are served, but even such treats as these are being put aside for the Anglo sweet pastries and drinks. Hopi corn puddings and breads, and roasted game meats are served when visitors come for a feast.

The Hopis are a proud people and value their long and productive heritage. They have treated their land with respect and it has nourished them well. In time, they will rely less on the land and more on commercial enterprise for the production of food—as they are already doing. Nonetheless, the early Hopi ways were good ways and should be preserved for the generations still to come.

A Guide to Unusual Foods

Some of the ingredients in the recipes that follow are unique to the Hopi culture (and, in some instances, other Native American groups) and are difficult, if not impossible, to buy in ordinary markets. However, there are specialty houses such as longtime merchant

Peter Casados
Box 852
San Juan Pueblo, New Mexico 87566

and the

El Molina Mills
3060 West Valley Boulevard
Alhambra, California

that accept mail-order requests. The Hopi Culture Center in Oraibi, Arizona, is another possible source of information.

A few of the more unusual foods are:

1. *Blue Cornmeal* — the pulverized kernels of a variety of corn that is blue in color. Commercially ground white or yellow cornmeal can be substituted, but there will be a change in color and flavor, and the authenticity of the original will certainly be challenged. Commercially ground cornmeal should be further pulverized in a blender or food mill when corn flour or finely ground cornmeal is called for.

2. *Culinary Ashes* — the charred remains of certain plants. Hopis prefer to use the four-winged saltbush (chamisa) because of its ability to color foods blue, a color that is religiously significant to them. Culinary ashes can be omitted from a recipe without noticeable change in taste but with a loss in mineral content. An equivalent amount of water should be substituted for the ash water that is omitted.

3. *Corn Husks* — the shucks from fresh corn. Corn husks can be saved and dried or purchased in some markets, although Hopi corn has longer husks than most commercially grown hybrid corn. Parchment paper or aluminum foil can be used in place of husks.
4. *Nanakopsie* — a native plant, commonly called bee balm, that is gathered and dried by the Hopi women for use as a seasoning in meats and stews. There is no substitute, but other herbs such as thyme or sage will give good flavor to the recipes. The Indians also use garlic, onions, oregano, coriander, and black pepper as seasonings.
5. *Tepary Beans* — a variety of small bean that grows wild in the Southwest and is prized by the Indians for its good taste and reputed high food value. Other small beans, such as navy beans, can be used, but there will be a change in flavor.
6. *Tuitsma* — another wild plant, called chinchweed, that is picked in late summer for its flowers and leaves, which are used for seasoning.

Beans

Nutrition in a Pod

One of the most appetizing aromas in the world is a pot of well-seasoned beans bubbling on the back of a warm kitchen stove on a cold winter's day. Gourmets tend to scoff at the lowly bean—but unrightly so. With its high quantities of protein and carbohydrates, vitamins and minerals, it has kept many a low-income family alive and has been a staple in the Indian diet, probably for as long as they have known about it.

No one is certain when or how the various types of beans were introduced on the Hopi Reservation, but it is assumed that they were traded as commodities with other Indians or brought in as gifts from foreign travelers. At least fourteen different types are grown in the various bean fields on the reservation, and others are still gotten through trade or are purchased. The Hopis eat the beans fresh or, more often, dry them for later use. (The women prefer fresh beans, however, as older beans take longer to cook.)

Teparies are delectable and nourishing little beans that grow wild in southern Arizona but have been cultivated by some Indian groups also. The Hopis have grown the little white teparies for a long time, and a wise old Hopi woman told me that it is necessary to plant three for the table and two for the rabbits to be sure of getting a good harvest. There are black teparies, with veined and wrinkled surfaces, and light brown teparies with reddish-brown or reddish-purple mottling, as well as the white.

Various types of string beans are also grown on the reservation, including cream, purple, red, and the blue ones that are used to dye basket materials. Green beans are strung on yucca fiber and dried, the only beans the Hopis store and eat in the pod. The common kidney bean is a variety of the red string bean, and the popular and tasty pinto is another variety of string bean. Besides using them for food, the Indians also make a bean paste, which they use instead of pine pitch to anchor turquoise in jewelry.

[3]

Lima beans are not cooked as often as string beans and teparies, but make a nice change in the menu. Limas also come in different shades, from white to cream to light brown, to brighter yellows, reds, and blacks.

Beans were once cooked in pottery pots, but long cooking frequently wore the bottoms out of these pots, and they were relegated for use as chimneys. Most housewives in the seventies were simmering their beans in metal pots or the slow cookers that are so ideal for foods of this kind. Some were using pressure cookers and others were even pressure canning beans, for maximum storage. Beans do not keep well, so, when refrigeration is not available, Hopi women keep them simmering for a day or two on the back of their stoves, until their families can eat them. Beans will keep in a refrigerator for up to a week, and in a freezer for six months or longer.

Drying Beans

Beans are dried in their pods on the vines. When the pods have fully matured and the vines or bushes have become dry and brittle, they are pulled out of the ground and carried home. The dried vines are piled up on canvases and the women hold a "work party," to shell the beans and winnow the pods for foreign matter. The vines and pods are then burned, and the residue is used for culinary ashes.

The shelled beans are spread out on clean cloths to dry, which takes a number of days depending on the amount. When all the moisture has evaporated from the beans, they are poured into barrels or sacks and stowed away in storage houses until needed.

Cooking Beans

Dried beans can be soaked or not, but take less time to cook if they have been presoaked. One method is to wash and sort the beans, cover them with water, and allow them to soak overnight in a cool place. The next day they can be cooked in the same water until tender.

An alternate method is to wash and sort the beans, cover them with cold water, and bring them to a boil, in a covered kettle. Boil for two minutes, remove the kettle from the heat, and let the beans stand—tightly covered—for one hour. Then simmer the beans in the same water until tender.

One cup of dried beans will expand to two or more cups when cooked. Different varieties can be substituted for each other in most recipes.

HOPI PINTO BEANS

2 1/2 cups dried pinto beans   1 cup bacon or a piece of ham
7 cups water   salt to taste

1. Wash and sort beans carefully.
2. Put beans in a bean pot or large saucepan and add bacon or ham and 7 cups of water.
3. Simmer for three hours or until beans are tender, stirring occasionally and adding hot water as needed.
4. Add salt to taste. (The amount will vary according to the quantity of salt in the meat and individual preference.)
5. Serve as a main meal with tortillas and a green vegetable, or as a light meal with fried bread.

Traditional bean pots have given way to pressure cookers in many Hopi kitchens. This recipe can be pressure cooked for forty-five minutes at fifteen pounds pressure. Cool until pressure drops to zero, then remove lid and simmer the beans for an additional twelve minutes.

CHILE BEANS

[Serves Six to Eight]

1/2 to 1 pound ground beef   1 teaspoon garlic powder
  (more if desired)   1 tablespoon salt
1 medium onion, chopped   2 cups dried pinto beans
1 tablespoon chile powder   water as needed
  or crushed chile

1. Brown meat in a skillet.
2. Add chopped onion and sauté slowly until it is golden in color.
3. Stir in chile powder and other seasonings and remove from the fire.
4. Pick and wash beans, put them in a large pot, and cover with water.
5. Add meat mixture to the beans, cover, and simmer for three hours, or until the beans are soft. Stir occasionally to keep the beans from burning, and add hot water as necessary.
6. Serve with fried bread, whole wheat tortillas, or someviki.

REFRIED BEANS

1/4 cup shortening
  (bacon or ham drippings
  are good)
1/4 cup grated cheese

1 teaspoon salt
1 cup cooked beans that have
  been mashed

1. Melt shortening in a skillet.
2. Add mashed beans and salt to melted shortening and cook over medium heat until the beans are saturated with shortening—five or ten minutes. Stir frequently to prevent beans from burning.
3. Add cheese and cook a minute or two longer, to melt the cheese.

Refried beans are probably of Mexican origin but have become a popular dish in Indian diets also.

PINTO BEANS AND HOMINY

3 cups dried pinto beans
10 cups water
1 tablespoon salt
1/2 cup diced salt pork

3 cups hominy
  (prepared according to
  directions on page 35)

1. Wash and sort beans, and put them into a cooking pot.
2. Stir in water, salt, and diced salt pork.
3. Cover and simmer slowly for two hours, until beans are almost tender.
4. Rinse partially cooked hominy to remove ash and add to beans.
5. Simmer, covered, for another hour, or until beans and hominy are well done.
6. Serve as a main dish, with a side dish of chile or native greens and tortillas or fried bread. Or serve as a vegetable with another main dish.

BAKED SWEET CORN AND PINTO BEANS

2 cups dried pinto beans	12 cups water
3 cups shelled baked	1 cup diced salt pork
sweet corn	or ham
(see page 22)	1 tablespoon salt

1. Wash and sort beans, and put into a cooking pot.
2. Shell corn, wash it, and add to the beans.
3. Add water, salt pork or ham, and salt.
4. Cover and simmer three hours, or until beans and corn are tender, stirring occasionally and adding hot water as needed.
5. This recipe can also be cooked in a pressure cooker. Cook at fifteen pounds pressure for fifty minutes, then remove from heat until mixture cools and pressure is reduced. Remove lid and return beans to heat, to simmer for fifteen minutes. This removes the pressure cooked flavor, which some people find objectionable.

The Spaniards introduced fruit, wheat, sheep, and pork to the Hopis. Pork products are used to season many dishes—either as salt pork, a slice of ham, or ham bone. Although a few pigs are raised on the reservation, most Hopi housewives get their meat products at local supermarkets.

PINTO BEANS WITH WATERMELON SEEDS

1/2 cup watermelon seeds   1/2 tablespoon salt
1 cup dried pinto beans   3 cups boiling water

1. Spread dry watermelon seeds on a cookie sheet and roast in a 300°F oven for ten to twelve minutes, or until golden brown and crisp. Stir occasionally to keep seeds from burning.
2. When seeds have cooled, grind them to a fine meal in a hand grinder.
3. Pour seed meal into a sieve with a fine mesh, and place the sieve over a large bowl. Pour the boiling water over the meal until most of the seed meal is washed from the hull. Save the liquid to pour on the beans.
4. Wash and sort beans and put them in a saucepan or bean pot. Add the liquid from the seed meal and cover and simmer for three hours, or until beans are tender. Stir occasionally and add hot water as needed. (The beans can also be pressure cooked for forty-five minutes at fifteen pounds pressure.)

This recipe was used during times of famine when drippings and meat were scarce. The watermelon seeds lend a nutty flavor to the beans.

DRIED BOILED BEAN SAUCE (Tuma Wutaka)

1 cup finely ground beans that   Seasonings to taste
  have been cooked and dried   (chile, pepper, onions, etc.)
2 cups water

1. Combine beans and water in a saucepan and simmer for twenty minutes, stirring often.
2. Add seasonings or meat drippings to taste.
3. Serve with chopped, raw onions and someviki for a light meal. (This recipe can also be used as a sauce or gravy, as a bean dip, or for making refried beans.)

During years of drought or other hard times on the reservation, food is never wasted. Leftover cooked beans are drained and spread out to dry, then are carefully stored for future use. Any cooked beans can be preserved in this way, but pinto beans are the most common.

HOPI DRIED STRING BEANS

[Serves Four to Six]

1 string of dried string beans
   (approximately 1 pound)
3 quarts water

1/4 pound cubed salt pork
1 tablespoon salt

1. Wash beans to remove dust.
2. Soak beans for thirty minutes in 3 quarts of water.
3. Add salt and salt pork to beans and simmer for three hours, or until beans are tender.
4. Stir occasionally and add hot water as needed.

This recipe adds variety to the Hopi diet and is quite tasty. The mature bean pods are cooked and served whole and are eaten with the fingers. When you put a bean into your mouth, you hold onto the end of the pod and draw the bean forward between your teeth to remove the string. The strings are then deposited on the rim of the plate.

LIMA BEANS WITH PORK

[Six Servings]

2 cups dried lima beans
water, to cover
3/4 pound salt pork
1 1/4 cups tomato juice

1 small onion, chopped
1/8 teaspoon chile powder
1 teaspoon garlic salt

1. Wash and sort beans, cover with water, and soak for several hours or overnight.
2. Add salt pork to the beans, and cover and simmer in the same water until beans are tender.
3. Add tomato juice, onion, garlic, and chile powder and continue cooking until beans are very tender and broth is thick.
4. While cooking, stir beans occasionally and add hot water as needed.

Lima beans are not an everyday bean but are cooked when the homemaker craves them or to give variety to the diet. They can be served as a main dish or as a vegetable.

Corn

A Gift From Mother Earth

Corn, whether growing in lush green fields or hanging in colorful dried clusters from the roof rafters, is more than food to the Hopi people — it is life. At the naming ceremony of the newborn, a special ear of corn is selected as the "mother corn" and is held sacred by the family, until it is used much later as food. Some families also put a taste of blue cornmeal into the baby's mouth, saying, "This corn is your life's strength. Eat this and grow strong and have a long, happy life."

Corn has been the focal point of Hopi culture and religion for as long as anyone remembers and is used in every ceremony. Hopi corn is a pure, ancient strain that can be planted as deep as eighteen inches, where it can reach water for germination, and still produce a shoot that is strong enough to reach the surface. Seeds are selected with great care and are considered the property of the matrilineal household. In the past, they were scarce, and therefore precious, and were stored in special pottery jars that were covered with flat stones to keep out rodents. Then they were planted in several fields, so that if one field was destroyed by floods or other natural causes, there was a chance that others would be spared.

Hopi corn has twelve rows of kernels and comes in a variety of colors including white, blue, red, yellow, and speckled. White corn is the major crop on the reservation and is used for flour, hominy, tamales, and prayer offerings. Blue corn, varying from gray to almost black in color, is the second most important crop and is used mainly in breads, sauces, and drinks. Recent studies indicate that it may have more food value than other varieties, and therefore may help to prevent malnutrition diseases among low-income Indian groups. Red corn, in shades of pink to maroon, is used for parched corn, and in earlier times was used for dye. Yellow corn is often substituted for white corn in both cooking and in ceremonies.

Sweet corn, best known as corn-on-the-cob, is also grown on the reservation or purchased. The first ears of fresh sweet corn are brought into the villages in late July at the time of the final Kachina dance, the Home Dance. Early in the morning on the day of the Home Dance, the many-hued Niman Kachinas bring in stalks of sweet corn with little gifts attached and present them to the unitiated children, introducing them to these perfect spirit-beings that are so important in the Hopi religion. When the later crop comes in, Hopi families bake many ears of sweet corn and dry them on the cob for use during the winter months. Hopi baked corn retains more nitrogen, potassium, and essential trace minerals than corn dried in other ways. Corn is generally stored on the cob to protect it from insects, which are more apt to get into shelled corn.

When the corn is harvested in the fall, it is brought into the villages, dried on the roof tops, and stacked in colorful rows in the yards. It looks as if the houses are surrounded by brightly colored fences and is a beautiful sight indeed. How secure Hopi families feel at the end of every harvest, knowing they have a new supply of corn. It's like money in the bank. Over the course of a year an average, five-member family will use about twelve bushels of corn per person for regular meals, fifteen bushels for ceremonies, and another fifteen for weddings.

While the corn is drying, it must be turned frequently to ensure fast, thorough drying. When the men are working in the fields and drying the corn, the women of the house trim off the husks and bundle and tie them with yucca or corn husk strips, to be used for cooking containers later. All the old corn must then be removed from the storage bins and the bins cleaned and plastered for the new corn. The old corn will not be thrown away but will be placed in the storage areas last so it will be used before the new corn, a system of supply rotation that has always been practiced by the Hopis.

Corn remains first in Hopi agriculture but is dependent for growth on summer rains and faith that the Creator will provide the needed moisture. Older families, who remember hard times, try to hold back a one- or two-year supply of corn, in case of crop failure.

Grinding Corn

Since Hopi women regularly prepare more than thirty different corn dishes, cornmeal is a staple that needs to be prepared and kept on hand at all times. In previous decades, corn was ground on grinding stones. Three stones usually rested side-by-side in the home, the first for very coarse meal, the second for medium ground meal, and the third for fine meal or flour. The maternal grandmother started teaching young girls to grind corn at an early age, so they would be able to grind without assistance during the puberty ceremony, and to prepare them for their eventual roles as homemakers and mothers.

Corn grinding often turned into a social occasion, when a group of girls gathered to grind while an uncle or grandfather sang. The girls would grind to the rhythm of the song. A small window was often located next to the grinding stones and provided a safe way for a boy to court a girl while she was grinding. If the maiden was interested in the young man, they would visit through the window. But, if she wanted to discourage him, she would fling cornmeal at him.

Special shelves were built above the grinding area so that the amount of cornmeal on hand could be seen at a glance. A young girl's diligence was judged by the amount of cornmeal in the home. The industrious maiden was (and still is) much sought after, as she was a basic necessity to the family.

Some Hopi women, especially the older ones, still use stones to grind corn—some of them handed down for many generations. But many are succumbing to the more convenient hand mills or electric blenders. Yellow corn is usually purchased at the grocery store, but most Hopi women still grind their own white and blue corn, by whatever method. Stone-ground corn can be purchased at a few select markets as harina azul (for tortillas), harina para atole (for gruel), or, unground, as posole (for hominy).

MAKING BLUE CORN FLOUR

1. Shell dried blue corn.
2. Wash corn until the water runs clear.
3. Coarsely grind corn in a hand-powered corn mill.
4. Put ground corn in a shallow pan and bake at 350°F until the corn puffs and smells like popcorn—about twenty minutes.
5. Remove corn from pan and cool.
6. Grind puffed corn on grinding stones or in a food mill until it is as fine as flour.
7. Store cornmeal in a covered container in a cool place.

Blue corn flour is available commercially as harinella, but this product is a mixture of blue and white cornmeals so it doesn't have as strong a flavor and color as pure blue cornmeal.

GRUEL

3 1/2 cups water   1 teaspoon salt (omit for fasting)
1 1/4 cups blue cornmeal

1. Bring water to a boil.
2. Mix cornmeal and salt together.
3. Pour boiling water over the cornmeal and mix well.
4. Return gruel to stove and heat slowly—stirring constantly.
5. Cook slowly, continuing to stir, for about five minutes, or until smooth and thick.

Gruel is served to patients on soft diets and is often requested by older Hopis when they are hospitalized. Many hospitals in the Southwest serve Indian foods to patients on request.

HOPI OMELETTE

[Serves Four]

1 dozen fresh eggs, warmed to room temperature	4 tablespoons shortening or drippings
3/8 cup finely ground blue cornmeal	seasonings, as desired

1. Beat 10 eggs until light and frothy.
2. Gradually add blue cornmeal to eggs, while continuing to beat. Add seasonings.
3. Slightly stir 2 remaining eggs and fold into mixture.
4. Heat shortening in heavy skillet or pan with deep sides, coating it thoroughly.
5. Pour egg mixture into hot pan and bake at 400°F for ten minutes. Reduce heat to 350°F and continue baking until eggs are firm but still fluffy (fifteen to twenty minutes).

Mrs. Josephine James
Hotevilla, Arizona

HOMINY AND EGGS

2 cups drained, cooked hominy (see page 35)	1 tablespoon shortening
4 well-beaten eggs	seasonings, as desired

1. Melt shortening in a skillet.
2. Brown hominy in the shortening over medium heat.
3. Stir beaten eggs into hominy and add seasonings.
4. Cook until eggs are set and ready to serve, stirring constantly to prevent scorching.

Hominy and eggs make a good breakfast or supper dish, especially when served with green chili strips.

BLUE MARBLES

[Serves One]

2 heaping teaspoons chamisa
  or other cooking ash
8 tablespoons boiling water

1/2 cup finely ground blue
  cornmeal
1 tablespoon sugar (if desired)

1. Mix the chamisa ash with 2 tablespoons of boiling water and set aside.
2. Measure the blue cornmeal and sugar into a bowl and stir in 5 tablespoons of boiling water.
3. Pour 2 tablespoons or more of the ash-water mixture through a strainer into the cornmeal, until the dough is distinctly blue in color.
4. Shape dough into balls the size of marbles.
5. Drop balls into 2 cups of boiling water and cook for ten minutes.

Blue marbles are served in a bowl in their cooking water along with dried onions, fresh or dried chiles, fried salt pork, or strips of beef. This is usually a breakfast dish and is a complete meal.

Mrs. Phyllis Adams
Polacca, Arizona

BLUE CORNMEAL AND FLOUR GRIDDLE CAKES

[Approximately Twelve 3-inch Cakes]

1/2 cup finely ground
  blue cornmeal
1/2 cup all-purpose flour
1/4 cup dry milk

1 tablespoon baking powder
2 tablespoons shortening
1 cup warm water

1. Combine dry ingredients and stir.
2. Melt shortening in water and add to dry ingredients, beating well.
3. Drop by spoonfuls onto a lightly greased, hot griddle and cook until golden brown on both sides. Turn once.

BLUE CORNMEAL HOTCAKES

[Twelve 3-inch Cakes]

1 cup blue cornmeal
1 tablespoon baking powder
1 teaspoon salt
1 tablespoon sugar

3 tablespoons melted shortening
2 eggs, beaten
1 cup milk (or 1/4 cup milk
   powder plus 1 1/4 cups water)

1. In a large mixing bowl, combine dry ingredients (including powdered milk if you are using it). Stir ingredients together.
2. Add shortening, eggs, and liquid and mix well.
3. Drop by spoonfuls on a lightly greased griddle, turning once as cakes brown—usually three to four minutes.

MUMUOZPIKI

[Serves Four]

2 heaping teaspoons chamisa ash
4 tablespoons boiling water

1 cup coarse-ground blue cornmeal
1/2 cup boiling water

1. Mix chamisa ash with 4 tablespoons of boiling water and set aside.
2. Mix cornmeal with 1/2 cup of boiling water.
3. Strain ash water through cheesecloth into cornmeal mixture until mixture turns blue (too much will make mixture turn green).
4. When mixture cools, knead it for three minutes.
5. Break off dough, a tablespoon at a time, and squeeze it tightly in hand to shape it.
6. Drop shaped rolls into a quart of boiling water and simmer for ten minutes.

This is a breakfast dish.

BLUE TORTILLAS

1 cup crushed piki (when piki   1/8 teaspoon salt
    is used, no ashes are needed)   (more if desired)
1/2 cup finely ground,   1 cup boiling water
    packed corn flour

1. Combine first three ingredients in a mixing bowl.
2. Gradually stir in boiling water and knead dough until smooth.
3. Divide dough into four 2-inch balls.
4. Flatten balls by hand to 1/4-inch thickness. Work cracks with a wet finger to smooth and seal.
5. Cook on a lightly greased griddle approximately four minutes on each side. Continue to smooth tortillas with wet fingers as they are cooking.

This recipe makes four 3 1/2-inch tortillas that are very good when served with beans.

CORN TORTILLAS

[Twelve Tortillas]

2 cups blue cornmeal
1 1/4 cups water

1. Mix cornmeal and water until dough is pliable and moist (but not sticky or wet).
2. Shape dough into twelve balls.
3. Flatten balls by patting out with hands or rolling between two sheets of greased wax paper.
4. Cook on lightly greased griddle over medium heat about four minutes on each side, or until brown.

In the past, Hopis either had to mine their own rock salt near Zuni or the Grand Canyon, or had to trade for it, and it was so difficult to obtain that it was almost a delicacy. Salt gathering, therefore, is a very special ceremony. Consequently, many early recipes, such as this one, didn't call for salt. Actually, the flavor of blue corn is so delicate that some cooks don't like to interfere with it by adding salt.

MODERN-DAY TORTILLAS

1 1/2 cups masa harina
2 teaspoons salt

2 teaspoons shortening
1 1/4 cups boiling water

Also:
2 pieces white muslin,
  six-inches square

2 heavy cutting boards

1. Mix salt and masa harina.
2. Melt shortening in boiling water and add to dry ingredients.
3. Using a pastry blender or mixer, beat mixture well for ten minutes.
4. Dampen the muslin and lay a square on one of the cutting boards.
5. Pinch off one piece of dough at a time and roll into a one-inch ball.
6. Place the ball on the muslin, top with the second piece of muslin, and flatten with the second cutting board. (The tortillas should be almost paper thin.)
7. Remove the board and peel off the muslin.
8. Cook the tortillas on a lightly greased griddle, turning once, until they are brown.

Masa harina is a special flour and cornmeal mixture for making tortillas. It can be purchased in specialty food shops, Spanish groceries, and even some supermarkets.

CORN AND FLOUR TORTILLAS

[*Twelve Tortillas*]

1/3 cup sifted all-purpose flour
1 2/3 cup blue cornmeal

1 cup water

1. Combine flour and cornmeal in a mixing bowl.
2. Stir in water and mix well.
3. Shape dough into twelve balls and roll them out between two sheets of greased wax paper (or pat them flat by hand).
4. Cook on a greased griddle or in a frying pan over medium heat, turning once, until lightly brown on both sides.

BAKING SWEET CORN

In September or October, when the sweet corn is ready to be harvested, families and friends gather together for the task of baking and drying the corn, to preserve it for use during the winter months.

The corn is baked in a deep pit in the ground, which is dug by the men in the family. Most pits are jug-shaped, and are approximately six feet deep and five feet across. Our pit is rectangular and only five feet deep and four across, but is six feet long. It will bake seventy ears of corn at a time.

While some of the men go out to the fields to gather the corn, others build a fire in the pit and keep it burning until late afternoon, and when the sand in the pit begins to change color then they know the pit is hot enough to bake the corn. They place a thick layer of green corn stalks over the hot coals, to keep the corn from burning, and then dump in the corn as quickly as possible. When all the corn has been placed in the pit, it is sprinkled with water (about eight cups for our pit), covered with metal, and the edges are sealed with a plaster of mud to hold in the steam.

The corn is steamed in the pit overnight, and early the next morning—about five or six o'clock—the mud plaster and metal lid are removed and the steam is allowed to escape for some fifteen or twenty minutes. Then the men take turns removing the hot ears of corn, and the rest of the family husks it. The short stems of the corn are pierced with an awl or ice pick, and the ears are strung together with yucca thread or wire in alternating directions, to keep the ears from touching and allow the air to circulate around them. After the thread or wire is tied, the corn is hung outside on rafters, to dry completely before being taken inside for storage.

Baking sweet corn in a pit is a method of preserving corn that Hopis have practiced for centuries and will probably continue to practice for time to come, despite the impact of technology on our culture. I don't know of a way that this method can be duplicated in the modern kitchen.

DRIED BAKED SWEET CORN

[*Serves Six*]

3 cups shelled,
   dried, baked sweet corn
1/2 cup bacon drippings

1 tablespoon salt
12 cups water

1. Wash and dry baked sweet corn and crack in a food chopper.
2. Put cracked corn in a saucepan and add water, salt, and drippings.
3. Cover and simmer for two hours or until corn is tender. Stir often to prevent scorching.
4. Serve as a vegetable or add to stews.

DRIED BAKED SWEET CORN STEW

Omit the drippings in the above recipe and add 2 pounds of stew meat. Cover and simmer for two hours or until corn and meat are tender.

FRESH CORN CHILE FRITTERS

3 cups fresh corn,
   scraped from the cob
1/4 cup chopped fresh chile

1 teaspoon salt
1 egg
shortening

1. Grind corn very fine with a hand meat grinder.
2. Add chile and salt to corn.
3. Mix in egg.
4. Cook on a greased griddle, as you would pancakes.

This dish can also be baked in a casserole, in a 350°F oven for thirty minutes, or until set. Fritters are served as a main dish or with plain meat stews.

SWEET CORN PUDDING (Pikami)

[Serves Fifty]

2 cups ground sprouted wheat
30 cups finely ground white
  or yellow cornmeal

16 cups boiling water
4 cups (approximately) sugar
  or honey, if desired

1. Sprout 6 cups of wheat until the shoots are 1 to 1 1/2 inches tall. Spread the sprouted wheat out to dry and grind it fine. This should yield approximately 2 cups of ground sprouted wheat. (Extra wheat can be stored in a jar for later use.)
2. Mix 2 cups of ground sprouted wheat with 30 cups of cornmeal.
3. Add approximately 16 cups of boiling water to make a heavy batter, and stir with a stirring stick until smooth.
4. Add sugar to taste and mix well.
5. Line a 10-quart container with dried corn husks.
6. Fill the container with pudding mixture.
7. Cover pudding with wet corn husks and aluminum foil, then put the lid on the container.
8. Lower pudding into preheated pudding pit and cover with pit cover. Seal the pit with wet mud.
9. Bake eight to ten hours or overnight in the pit of hot coals.
10. Early the next morning, open the pit carefully and stir the pudding.
11. Dip pudding out and serve warm with stew for breakfast.

A smaller amount of pudding can be made with 4 cups cornmeal, 1/4 cup ground sprouted wheat, 2 cups boiling water, and 1/2 cup sugar, but it is prepared and cooked in the same manner.

Stirring sticks are made from greasewood. Some are single sticks the size of a broom handle and others are made of four slender sticks (about 3/8 of an inch in diameter) tied together.

Mrs. Phyllis Adams
Polacca, Arizona

SWEET CORN PUDDING (MODERN VERSION)

5 pounds whole wheat flour   5 pounds granulated sugar
5 pounds white corn flour   10 to 14 cups boiling water

1. In a large pan (we keep a tub just for this purpose), combine whole wheat flour, corn flour, and sugar.
2. Add boiling water to the dry ingredients, a little at a time, stirring well to moisten all ingredients and make a thick pudding. (Three women, usually the in-laws, are needed to stir the pudding as it is very thick and hot.)
3. Test a small amount of pudding on a hot griddle. If it browns readily, the pudding is sweet enough. If not, more sugar should be added.
4. Prepare the cooking container (usually a 5-gallon can) by lining it with clean corn husks.
5. Dip a dipper into water and then into the pudding, and carefully pour the pudding into the bottom of the container. Continue to dip the dipper into water before dipping into the pudding, to help pudding slip off the dipper more easily.
6. When all the pudding has been put in the container, cover it with wet corn husks, aluminum foil, and a lid.
7. Lower the pudding into a hot pudding pit, cover it with the pit cover, and plaster it with wet mud, sealing the opening well.
8. Build a small fire over the pudding pit and cook the pudding overnight.

Hopi or Sweet Corn Pudding is served for breakfast on feast and dance days, and at weddings and the naming party for a new baby. It is not eaten with a spoon, but by breaking small pieces off and eating them with the fingers. Leftover pudding is dried and pulverized and made into a beverage by adding hot water.

The in-laws usually "trade off" for work at Hopi weddings. If a Hopi woman has a daughter, she will help her clan relatives at their daughters' weddings. They will then return the favor when her daughter gets married.

QUICK PIKAMI

3 cups piki crumbs (see page 29) 1/3 cup blue cornmeal
2 cups boiling water 2 tablespoons sugar

1. Add piki crumbs to boiling water and continue to boil, over moderate heat, until piki is tender—about five minutes. Stir frequently.
2. Add cornmeal slowly, stirring to mix well.
3. Cook for five more minutes, stirring constantly to prevent burning.
4. Add sugar and continue to cook, stirring constantly, for ten more minutes, or until pudding becomes very thick.
5. Serve with greens, stews, meats, or with stewed peaches.

This quick version of Sweet Corn Pudding is usually made in the daytime for a quick bread. Regular Pikami is cooked overnight in a pudding pit.

Phyllis Adams
Polacca, Arizona

BLUE CORN DUMPLINGS

[*Serves Four to Six*]

1 cup blue corn flour 1 teaspoon bacon drippings,
2 teaspoons baking powder lard, or other shortening
1 teaspoon salt 1/3 to 1/2 cup milk

1. Mix (or sift) dry ingredients thoroughly in a mixing bowl.
2. Cut in shortening and add enough milk to make a drop batter.
3. Drop by spoonfuls on top of stew.
4. Cover kettle and steam dumplings for fifteen minutes. Stew should be kept bubbling.

HOPI HUSH PUPPIES

[Serves Six]

2 cups blue cornmeal
1 teaspoon salt
2 teaspoons baking powder
2 beaten eggs

1 1/4 cups milk
1 small onion, chopped fine
shortening

1. Measure cornmeal, salt, and baking powder into a mixing bowl.
2. Stir milk into beaten eggs and gradually add to cornmeal mixture.
3. Add chopped onions to cornmeal and mix well.
4. Drop by teaspoonfuls into 1 1/2 inches of very hot shortening.
5. Fry hush puppies until golden brown, turning to brown all sides.

Hush puppies are served with stews or beans instead of bread. Although made of corn, they are corn in a different form and add variety to meals. Yellow cornmeal can be substituted for blue, but does not have as delicate a flavor.

WHOLE CORN AND BEAN SPROUTS (Hazruquive)

[Serves Eight to Ten]

6 ears dried white or speckled
   corn, broken into 3- or
   4-inch lengths
1 bunch bean sprouts

1 pound salt pork
   (or 1/2 cup pork drippings)
1/4 cup salt

1. Wash corn well to remove dust.
2. Put corn in a saucepan, cover it with water, and add salt and salt pork or drippings.
3. Cover saucepan and simmer corn until tender, usually overnight. (A crock pot is ideal for this.)
4. The next morning, wash bean sprouts until water runs clear, cut them in 1 1/2 inch lengths, and add to corn.
5. Cover and continue simmering until sprouts are tender and the kernels on the cobs pop—about three hours.
6. Serve with plain or chile piki.

This dish is a real specialty as it is prepared only once a year, during the Powamu Ceremony in late winter that celebrates the changing of the seasons. The corn cobs cooked with the other ingredients give the dish a deliciously sweet taste.

PIKI

Piki is a tissue-thin cornbread that is unique to the Hopi culture. It is served as crackers or wafers are served, often with onions and greens and a small dish of salt water on the side to dip the piki in. It is also served as a snack with tea or coffee, or carried for lunch when members of the family are working away from home.

Piki comes in different flavors and colors. Chile piki is particularly good with bean sprouts and stews, for example, and piki made from red or yellow corn is strung and given to children and friends at the summer Kachina dances. There is also a fresh corn piki, but it is seldom made or served.

Hopi women and girls make piki, as they have for centuries, on specially prepared cooking stones called piki stones. These stones must be a certain size and shape, and must also be very smooth. They take a long time to prepare, and most piki stones are heirlooms that have been handed down from mother to daughter for generations.

Piki-making is a hot demanding task and I didn't learn how until the summer of 1978, when a lady from New Oraibi invited me to her home for lessons. I took her up on her offer and went to her house every week to make piki. One of the first things I learned was that you must be determined to learn the art of piki-making—for it is indeed an art—as it would be very easy to give up after touching the hot stone for the first time! It was awe inspiring for me to see the piki batter sizzle right behind my unprotected hand.

But I enjoyed being in the piki house, for I found it to be a center of activity. The "moccasin grapevine" was headquartered there, and it was also a place for family counseling.

During the lessons, my teacher built the fire under her piki stone, for she knows her stone just as any good homemaker knows her cooking range. But I usually mixed the ingredients, while she continually encouraged me. Piki-making cannot be learned in one lesson but is a skill that comes with practice.

MAKING PIKI

3 tablespoons chamisa ash   8 cups boiling water
1/2 cup cold water   6 to 8 cups cold water
6 cups finely ground cornmeal

1. Mix chamisa ash with 1/2 cup of cold water and set aside.
2. Put cornmeal in piki bowl, pushing a third of the meal to the back of bowl.
3. Pour 4 cups of boiling water into the larger amount of cornmeal and stir with a wooden spoon or stirring stick until well blended. Add the rest of the boiling water and continue to mix until the larger amount of cornmeal is moistened. (The dough should be heavy and stiff.)
4. Strain ash water through broom straws or a sieve lined with cheesecloth into the dough, a little at a time, until dough turns blue. (Too little ash water is better than too much as you can always add more. If you do use too much, then add another cup of meal from the remaining cornmeal in the bowl and another cup of water.)
5. When dough is cool enough to handle, knead it by hand until the lumps are dissolved. Add extra meal, a little at a time, until all the cornmeal in the bowl is blended in.
6. Set dough aside and build a fire under the piki stone.
7. While the stone is heating, begin adding the cold water to the dough, a little at a time, and continue working dough with your hands. Add enough water to make a smooth, thin batter that is the consistency of crepe batter or thinner. The thinner the batter, the easier it is to work with, but some Hopi women prefer thicker batters. As you are making the piki, it may be necessary to add more cold water, since the batter has a tendency to thicken.
8. Wipe off the hot stone and oil it with either bone marrow or cooked brains, which will make the stone as slick as glass. The stone may require additional oiling after cooking two or three sheets in order to prevent sticking.
9. Dip your hand in the batter and hold a small amount in the curve of your fingers. Spread batter across the stone (touching the stone lightly with your fingers), moving from right to left and back again, and removing any lumpy deposits. Dip fingers into batter again to cool them—one has to work fast to avoid burning the fingers—and continue spreading batter across the stone, overlapping the previous strip, until stone is completely covered.

10. When piki is done, the edges will separate from the stone. With both hands, gently lift it from the stone and place it on the piki tray. (The first piece is "fed to the fire." Also at this time, the stone is asked "not to be lazy and to work well" for the cook.)
11. Spread more batter onto the stone and, while it is cooking, gently lift the sheet of piki from the piki tray back onto the stone and let it sit for a minute or two to soften. Then fold the two ends of the piki a quarter of the way toward the center and gently roll the piki away from you, as you would a cinnamon roll. Place rolled piki back on tray.
12. Lift the sheet still on the stone to the piki tray and spread the stone with more batter. Continue to bake and roll the piki until all batter is used.

If a sheet of piki tears when you are removing it from the stone, it may be put back into the bowl, where it will dissolve into the batter, to be used again. Or, if children are in the area, they will be glad to sample your failures!

THUMBPRINT BREAD (Kolatquvi)

[Serves Six]

2 teaspoons chamisa ash
1/4 cup water
2 cups coarse cornmeal

1 cup boiling water
1 tablespoon sugar

1. Mix ashes and 1/4 cup water and set aside.
2. Measure cornmeal and sugar into a mixing bowl.
3. Add 1 cup boiling water to cornmeal mixture and stir with a wooden spoon.
4. Strain ash water into cornmeal and stir until mixture turns blue.
5. Shape heaping tablespoons of dough into 1 1/2 inch balls. Indent the center of each ball with your thumb.
6. Put the thumbprint bread in a colander and set it in a pot of boiling water.
7. Cover pot and simmer bread for approximately eight minutes.

Some Hopi women divide the cornmeal mixture in half and add the boiling water to one side only, working the remainder of the cornmeal into the dough with their hands. This gives them more control when they add ash water to color the dough. Before colanders were available, Hopi housewives used dried peach twigs to make piki trays and other similar cooking utensils.

HOPI FINGER BREAD (Huzusuki)

[Serves Six]

1 3/4 cups blue cornmeal,   2 cups water
  ground medium fine

1. Bring water to a boil, then reduce heat to low.
2. Gradually add cornmeal to boiling water, stirring constantly. Stir until all cornmeal is mixed in. (This makes a very stiff dough.)
3. Spoon bread out onto a plate and serve.

Finger Bread, as the name implies, is eaten with the fingers. Each person breaks off a piece, using the thumb and first finger to hold it, and butters it or not before eating. Finger Bread is served often, especially with roasted meats and stews, and leftover bread is sliced and served for breakfast the next morning. Older Hopi women stirred the thick dough with a stirring stick, but a cooking fork dissolves the lumps more quickly.

Mrs. Remalda Lomayeatewa
Second Mesa, Arizona

USING LEFTOVER HUZUSUKI

Soup

4 cups water   1/2 cup meat drippings
1 cup leftover huzusuki   or chopped meat (more or less
salt   can be added according to taste)

1. Bring water to a rolling boil.
2. Crumble huzusuki into bite-size pieces and add to boiling water.
3. Add meat drippings and salt to taste.
4. Simmer until soup thickens.

By adding more water, you can make this same dish into a delicious and nourishing drink.

Hotcakes

1. Put leftover huzusuki into a loaf pan and chill.
2. Slice huzusuki into 1/4-inch slices and dip in beaten egg.
3. Fry slices in hot shortening until brown on both sides — approximately two minutes on each side.
4. Serve with syrup or jelly.

SOMEVIKI

[*Serves Eight*]

5 rounded tablespoons chamisa
  or other cooking ash
1 1/2 cups boiling water

1 cup finely ground blue cornmeal
3/4 cup granulated sugar
4 cups boiling water

Also:
30 corn husks that have been
  soaked in very hot water
  for ten to fifteen minutes

1. Mix ashes with 1 1/2 cups of boiling water and set aside.
2. Measure cornmeal and sugar into a bowl.
3. Add 4 cups of boiling water to dry ingredients, stirring constantly.
4. Pour a cup or more of ash water through a strainer into dough, until dough is distinctly blue in color.
5. Put 2 heaping tablespoons of dough on each corn husk and fold husks around dough, sides first and then ends. Secure with strings made from corn husks.
6. Drop husk-wrapped dough into a large pot of boiling water. Cover and simmer for twenty to twenty-five minutes, and drain.

Someviki is a sweet cornbread that is served hot, usually with beans or stew. The husks are carefully unwrapped from around the bread and discarded. Most people eat several pieces with a meal.

Mrs. Olive Dennis
Oraibi, Arizona

SPOONS FROM CORN HUSKS

Some early Hopi families had spoons made from gourds, but many did not. On dance and feast days, when there were not enough spoons for all the visitors, the ingenious Hopi would take the moist corn husks from the someviki, tie knots in the tips, and make useable spoons. The corn husks need to be soft and pliable in order to be twisted and tied in a knot, and, since boiled someviki is usually served with the stews and beans on feast days, the corn-husk wrappings were ideal.

CHUKUVIKI

5 rounded tablespoons chamisa
   or other cooking ash
1 1/2 cups boiling water
3/4 cups sugar

2 cups finely ground
   dark blue cornmeal
4 cups boiling water

Also:
3 dozen corn leaves that have
   been soaked in water and the
   water shaken off of them

1. Mix ashes with 1 1/2 cups of boiling water and set aside.
2. Combine cornmeal and sugar in a large mixing bowl.
3. Add 4 cups of boiling water and stir until blended.
4. Strain ash water through a cloth.
5. Add about 1 cup of ash water to cornmeal mixture, until it turns distinctly blue in color.
6. Knead dough until ash water is mixed in well. (Dough will be very thick.)
7. Wrap 2 tablespoons of dough in each corn leaf, securing with additional corn leaves as necessary.
8. Drop leaf-wrapped dough into a large pot of boiling water. Cover and simmer for thirty minutes.

Chukuviki has a distinctive shape, something like a quarter moon. There is quite a trick to wrapping the dough to make the shape, and it is served at wedding ceremonies only.

Mrs. Phyllis Adams
Polacca, Arizona

FRESH CORN ROLLS (Nakviki)

6 ears fresh tender corn   1 teaspoon salt, if desired

1. Remove husks from corn by cutting off ends. Save larger husks and wash them. Remove silks from corn.
2. Cut corn from cob, scraping as much milk from the cob as possible.
3. Grind corn with the fine blade of a hand meat grinder. (An electric blender can be used also, but tends to separate the starch, so it is necessary to stir the corn well.)
4. Add salt and mix well.
5. Put a tablespoon of corn mixture into a clean husk. Fold the left edge of husk over corn, then the right edge. Finally, fold the tip end up towards the center.
6. Stand rolls upright, open side up, in a jelly roll or similar pan.
7. Bake in a preheated 325°F oven for thirty minutes, or until corn mixture is solid.
8. Serve as corn bread with stews, soups, or roasted meat.

Nakviki is quite versatile and can be split and browned in butter or oleo to make a delicious breakfast toast. It can also be sliced crosswise and scrambled with eggs, or dried for winter use.

DRYING FRESH CORN ROLLS (Nakviklokvu)

Remove corn husks from leftover corn rolls and split them lengthwise (or slice crosswise) to ensure quick drying. Put rolls in a sifter basket and place them in a window or other sheltered, sunny spot. Turn rolls two or three times a day for even drying, and, when completely dried, store them in a tightly covered container. Nakviklokvu will keep for a year in a tightly closed container.

In the 1970s, many Hopi homes still didn't have electricity, and a few didn't have iceboxes, so drying foods for future use was very necessary. Sifter baskets were loosely-woven, shallow baskets made of yucca, that allowed plenty of air circulation. They were also used for shaking dirt from beans, seeds, etc., and for winnowing the hulls from parched corn.

USING NAKVIKLOKVU

4 cups water
1 cup dried nakviklokvu pieces
1 teaspoon salt

2 tablespoons butter
   or bacon drippings

1. Bring water to a boil in a saucepan.
2. Add nakviklokvu pieces, salt, and butter.
3. Cover and simmer for one hour, or until nakviklokvu is soft. Stir frequently as corn rolls will stick, just as corn will.
4. Serve as a vegetable.

Nakviklokvu can also be added to stews or a pot of beans.

HOPI HOMINY

2 cups shelled, dried, white
   or speckled corn
10 cups water

1 cup chamisa or other
   cooking ash

1. Put corn and water in an enamel saucepan, cover, and bring to a boil.
2. When water boils, stir in the cooking ash. (The corn will turn yellow-orange.)
3. Cover and simmer corn until hulls become loose and corn turns white again. Stir occasionally and add water as needed.
4. Drain corn in a colander and rinse under cold running water, removing hulls with your fingers.
5. The hominy can be dried or pressure canned for use at a later date, or can be patted dry and frozen in suitable containers.

For more rapid processing of the hominy, larger amounts of ashes can be used. Regardless of the amount of ashes, however, the hominy must be processed in an enamel pot, as the ashes react with metal utensils.

HOMINY MADE WITH SODA

2 tablespoons baking soda   2 cups dried white corn
2 or more quarts cold water

1. In a cooking kettle, dissolve soda in water.
2. Add corn, making sure water covers corn.
3. Cover corn and bring to a rapid boil, then reduce heat and simmer for three hours or until the hulls rub off easily. Stir occasionally and add water as needed to keep corn covered.
4. Drain and rinse corn in a strainer or colander and rub kernels thoroughly to remove hulls.
5. For use at a later date, dry or freeze hominy. Otherwise, cover corn with fresh cold water and simmer for an additional four hours, or until corn is tender.

This recipe does not have the nutrition of the hominy made with ash.

HOPI COFFEE CREAMER

4 cups water   clean sand
2 cups shelled, dried white corn

1. Add corn to water in a saucepan and bring to a rapid boil, stirring occasionally when corn starts to boil.
2. Keep corn at a rolling boil until one kernel swells and pops.
3. Remove corn from heat and drain.
4. Spread corn on a clean cloth and allow to dry in the open air of your house for three or four days.
5. When corn has dried, parch it in hot sand (see page 103), or place it in a pan and heat it in a 350°F oven until it pops.
6. When corn has cooled sufficiently, grind it coarsely. (A hand corn or flour mill is ideal for this.)
7. Winnow corn to remove hulls by placing it in a wire strainer and tossing it in the air.
8. Grind corn again, this time with a finer blade so that it resembles commercial cornmeal.
9. Roast in a 350°F oven, stirring to prevent scorching, until corn is lightly browned.
10. When corn has cooled again, grind it into flour.
11. Store in air-tight containers in the refrigerator.

Wheat

Flour and Yeast Breads

Wheat was brought to America by the Spaniards, and was probably introduced to the Indians by missionaries who worked their way up into Arizona from Mexico. Although corn breads are still preferred by the Hopis, wheat breads are popular also and have become a mainstay in their diet. Homemakers on the reservation bake from eight to twenty-eight golden loaves a week, depending on the size of their families and whatever activities might be going on in the community. In many homes, a large washtub is reserved just for making bread.

Both dry yeast and compressed cakes are available commercially to these modern homemakers, but older Hopi women created their own yeast by cooking cornmeal, potatoes, and sugar together to make a stiff dough, then pressed it into a pan, and cut it into two-inch squares. The squares were then dried and stored in a covered container until needed. One square provided enough leavening for four loaves of bread.

Another method was to save part of each batch of dough, roll it thin and dry it, and put it away until time to bake again. The dried leftovers were either ground or soaked in water and then added to the new dough.

Making sponge bread was yet another way to make leavening for wheat breads, one that is still being used by some Hopi women in the seventies. Sponge is made by dissolving yeast in more water than usual and adding enough flour to make a thick batter. The batter is covered with a clean cloth and put in a warm, draft-free place to ferment. When the batter becomes spongy and foamy, it is added to other ingredients and allowed to rise as in standard bread recipes.

Following are some tips on making yeast breads that are light, crusty, and bound to please any family, Hopi or otherwise.

1. Soften dry yeast in warm water (110°F) and compressed yeast cakes in lukewarm water (85°F). Hot water will kill yeast and

[39]

prevent bread from rising; cold water will make bread take too long to rise.

2. Sugar is important in any yeast bread recipe as it is the raw material from which yeast makes the leavening gas. It also adds flavor and aids in the browning of the bread.

3. A small amount of salt is important too, to control the action of the yeast and add flavor.

4. Add all the flour you need to keep the dough from sticking to your hands when you mix the dough initially. Flour that is added later may leave dark streaks in the bread.

HOPI FRY BREAD (Wequivi)

[Serves Six to Eight]

4 cups white all-purpose flour   2 to 2 1/4 cups water
5 teaspoons baking powder   shortening, as needed
1 1/2 teaspoons salt

1. Mix flour, baking powder, and salt in a large bowl.
2. Gradually stir in water to make a soft dough.
3. Continue stirring until dough is smooth and shiny.
4. Cover bowl with a clean towel and set aside for thirty minutes.
5. Shape dough into 16 balls, about the size of an egg, and roll them on a lightly floured board to 1/2-inch thickness or less.
6. Pour shortening 1 1/2 inches deep in a heavy frying pan and heat until it is just before the smoking point.
7. Place dough into hot fat, turning with a fork when it has browned on one side until it is golden brown on both sides.
8. Drain on absorbent paper.

Mrs. Edna Adams and
Mrs. Stella Huma
Polacca, Arizona

FRIED BREAD (Variation)

4 cups all-purpose flour   2 to 2 1/2 cups water
4 teaspoons baking powder   1/4 cup shortening
2 teaspoons salt   1 pound lard

1. Sift dry ingredients into a mixing bowl.
2. Cut in 1/4 cup shortening.
3. Add enough water to make dough hold together.
4. Knead dough until it is well mixed and smooth.
5. Roll dough to 1/2-inch thickness and cut into squares or triangles.
6. Heat lard to 400°F in an electric frying pan, or to just below the smoking point in a heavy skillet.
7. Place squares of dough in hot fat, turning to brown on both sides.
8. Drain bread on absorbent paper.
9. Serve hot with beans, stews, or honey.

ADOBE BREAD

[Makes Two Loaves]

1 package dry yeast (1/4 ounce)
1/4 cup lukewarm water
2 tablespoons melted lard
  or shortening

1 teaspoon salt
4 1/2 cups all-purpose flour
1 cup cold water

1. Soften the yeast in 1/4 cup warm water in a large mixing bowl. Combine one cup cold water with melted shortening and salt. Add to yeast mixture.
2. Add the flour alternately with the water, sifting in the flour, a little at a time and beating well after each addition to make a smooth mixture. You will probably have to knead in the final cup of flour.
3. Shape the dough into a ball, place in a greased bowl, brush lightly with melted lard or shortening, cover with a dry cloth, and set in a warm place to rise—about one hour.
4. When the dough has doubled in bulk, punch it down and turn it onto a floured board and knead it for about five minutes. Divide dough into two equal parts and shape into two round loaves on a well-oiled board or greased baking tin.
5. Cover the loaves with a dry cloth, set in a warm place again, and let rise forty-five minutes.
6. Bake the bread in a 400°F oven for fifty minutes, or until loaves are lightly browned and sound hollow when thumped.
7. Cool and cut into wedges to serve.

This bread is often baked in large quantities in outdoor ovens. Hopi women make a social event out of breadmaking, getting together to share the chores and local gossip. The bread keeps well and can be frozen for longer storage, making quantity baking a practical matter.

HOPI WHEAT BREAD

Fill a small saucepan half full of warm water and dissolve 5 or 6 packages of active dry yeast in it. Set aside.

Meanwhile, empty 3/4 of a 25-pound bag of flour into a washtub, 1/2 handful of sugar, 1/4 handful of salt, and mix well with hands. Add three scoops of lard and rub it into the flour mixture with the finger tips until it is distributed evenly. (More lard can be added, if needed.) Now add the yeast and enough additional warm water to make a stiff dough. (Test water on your wrist to make sure it is lukewarm.) Work dough with your hands until all lumps are dissolved. Cover and set aside in a warm place to rise. Punch down with hands and knead until elastic. Form dough into loaves, let rise again, and bake.

This recipe will make approximately 24 to 26 average-size (about 1 pound) round loaves. Hopi women who own beehive-type outdoor ovens large enough to bake this quantity share this convenience with relatives and friends in exchange for one or two loaves of the bread.

FLOUR TORTILLAS

6 cups white all-purpose flour	2 tablespoons baking powder
1 tablespoon salt (optional)	2 to 3 cups warm water

1. Mix dry ingredients in a bowl.
2. Stir in warm water to make a smooth batter.
3. Bake on a moderately hot griddle as you would any tortilla, allowing 1/4 cup batter for each tortilla.

Flour tortillas are made frequently and are literally thrown together. Workers out in the fields or away from home on other jobs will often take them for lunch, cooking them over an open fire.

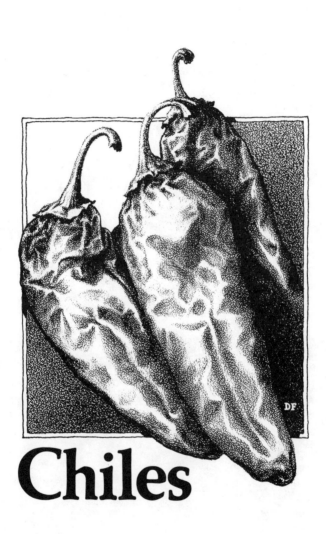

Chiles

Peppers With a Punch

With their first bite into a lucious-looking, bright red or green pod, most people develop respect for the power of a chile pepper. But in the Southwest, where a large variety of chiles ranging from mellow to campfire hot are grown and consumed with relish, the people have also learned to appreciate the rich, aromatic flavors these spicy plants give to so many foods. Chiles are more than just a seasoning, however. The red varieties, whether fresh, canned, or dried, are a good source of vitamin A, and all fresh chiles, no matter what their color, contain vitamin C. (Vitamin C is lost when chiles are dried.)

Chiles are regularly grown on the Hopi Reservation, mainly in terrace gardens below First Mesa where abundant spring waters flow just below the earth's surface and provide plenty of moisture. The women inherit the garden plots from their mothers and plant the peppers in late May, after the danger of frost has passed. By fall, strings of dried red and green peppers can be seen hanging in most Hopi homes—not as decoration, as in some Anglo homes, but as a very efficient means of preserving this popular seasoning.

Types of Chile Peppers

There are not only different types of chiles, including red, green, yellow, and dark green, but different regions grow chiles with their own distinctive flavors. Even chiles of the same variety and grown in the same field will vary in flavor and pungency, depending, apparently, on water availability and pollination.

The *Anaheim* is a long, green chile with thick flesh. It is one of the mildest of the chile peppers and, consequently, is one of the most popular. The *Cayenne* is also popular, but is much hotter and should be used sparingly. Orange-red in color, this pepper is usually dried and ground, and is readily available in most supermarkets. The *Chile Tepines* is another small, red pepper—about the size of a peanut— that is used mainly in hot sauces and to season other dishes. This pepper is usually dried also and is so hot that it is a good idea to use the back of a spoon to crush it, and then use it sparingly! The *Jalapeño* is short and dark green in color. It has particularly good flavor, but is very hot and should be used with caution. It is usually chopped fine and added to casseroles and salads. The *Hungarian Yellow Wax Chile* is one of several yellow wax varieties, some of which are long and tapering, others of which are short and conical. Their pungency also varies from sweet to very sharp. These chiles are eaten as relishes, made into pickles, or dried and added to sauces for extra spiciness. The *New Mexico* or *Río Grande* chile is similar to the *Anaheim* in that it is hot, green, and long in shape. It is grown in the Río Grande valley, north of Santa Fe, and is particularly prized by the Pueblo Indians of New Mexico. The *Pasilla* chile, also known as the *Poblano* or *Ancho,* has a heart-shaped pod and is black-green in color. It is dried and crushed or ground for chile sauces. The *Serrano* is considered the hottest chile of all. It is dark green and cylindrical like the *Jalapeño,* but is shorter and more slender. It is packed in oil or pickled, and is used mainly for hot pickles and sauces.

Selecting and Storing Chiles

Besides growing their own peppers, Hopi women also buy them from peddlars and in grocery stores. Mexican traders visit the reservation a couple of times a year, bringing various kinds of peppers to sell or trade, and the Hopis trade with other Pueblo Indians for such things as apples, cabbages, green tomatoes, onions, wheat, and, of course, chiles.

When buying chiles, it is important to select those with bright, vivid colors that are firm, shiny, and full fleshed. Wilted or flabby chiles, or chiles with cuts or punctures, are of poor quality. Soft spots indicate decay and can spoil the flavor of a chile.

There is no foolproof way of knowing how hot a chile is until you bite into it, but each variety has a certain range of mildness or sharpness. The heat of a chile is concentrated in the seeds, skins, and interior veins. Many cooks routinely remove the seeds and skin of a chile before using it, to assure a milder dish.

Hopi women traditionally grind their own chiles on grinding stones, and you will find a small bowl or shaker of red chili powder on most Hopi dining tables. But chiles can also be ground satisfactorily in a blender, and chile powder is available commercially as a blend of spices that includes ground red chiles, cumin seed and oregano, salt, powdered garlic, and occasionally, powdered onion.

Fresh chiles should be rinsed, to remove foreign matter, and patted dry, and should be stored in a cool place or refrigerated. Chile powder can be stored in the cupboard, but loses flavor and potency with time.

PEELING FRESH GREEN CHILES

1. Select enough fresh green chiles to serve your family—at least one per person.
2. Wash chiles and allow to dry, or wipe dry with a paper towel.
3. Put the chiles in a shallow pan and roast them in a 400°F oven, turning them so that all sides become blistered.
4. Steam the blistered chiles by placing a wet cloth on top of the pan for ten to fifteen minutes, or until the skin loosens and can be peeled easily.
5. When cool enough to handle, roll the chiles gently between the hands, further loosening the skins, then peel.
6. The peeled chiles may be frozen or canned for use at a later date. Or, they can be chopped or puréed in a blender.

Green chiles can be blistered over charcoal as well as on a stove or in an oven, but must be turned often—no matter where they are roasted—to prevent burning. They add interest to any dish and are served frequently by Hopi homemakers as a topping for eggs, a spread for sandwiches, or in stews.

If you plan to peel a large number of hot chiles, you should wear rubber gloves, as hot chiles contain capsaicin, a volatile oil that can cause burns. If you do handle chiles with your bare hands, avoid touching your face and eyes, and wash your hands thoroughly with soap and water as soon as you are finished. If your hands are irritated from the oil of the chiles, rub with any mild oil.

CHOPPED FRIED GREEN CHILES

1. Wash chiles and pat dry.
2. Cut chiles crosswise into 1/4-inch wide pieces. (Remove seeds for a milder dish.)
3. Melt 2 or 3 tablespoons of shortening in a skillet over medium heat.
4. When shortening is hot, carefully put in the sliced chiles.
5. Add seasonings to taste, such as garlic salt or other seasoned salt, and stir until chiles are light brown and crisp.
6. Serve hot with blue marbles, beans, eggs, or any meat dish.

FRIED GREEN CHILES

[Serves Six]

6 chile pods
3 tablespoons shortening

garlic salt

1. Wash chile pods and wipe dry.
2. Trim stems from pods.
3. With a sharp knife, make a 1-inch slit in the side of each pod, to keep it from popping and splattering when being fried.
4. Heat shortening in a heavy skillet and add chiles one at a time. Turn each chile, browning lightly on both sides.
5. Sprinkle chiles with garlic salt, and continue cooking until they are tender enough to be pierced with a fork.

Chiles in various forms add flavor to other foods, but by themselves they are delicious too. Fried green chiles are a favorite among the Hopi people.

FRIED DRIED RED CHILES

[Serves Six]

6 pods dried red chile
1 tablespoon shortening

1/4 teaspoon salt
1/2 teaspoon garlic salt

1. Wash chile pods and wipe dry. (Remove seeds for a milder dish.)
2. Crush or break dried chiles into quarter-inch pieces, and set aside.
3. Melt shortening in a small skillet over medium heat. Then turn the heat down, as dried chiles burn easily.
4. Add crushed chiles to the shortening and stir constantly until they are light brown. Add salt and garlic salt.
5. Serve hot with blue marbles, stews, or eggs.

PRESSURE CANNING GREEN CHILES

1. Select mature, unblemished, and freshly picked chiles.
2. Wash chiles carefully, to remove sand and other impurities.
3. Roast and steam the chiles to remove skins, according to the directions on page 49.
4. Remove stems and seeds.
5. Pack chiles in sterilized jars to within a half-inch of the top.
6. Add 1/2 teaspoon salt (optional) to half-pint jars, 1 teaspoon salt to pint jars.
7. Wipe rims of jars with a clean cloth or paper towel.
8. Put lids on jars and tighten.
9. Place jars on rack in canner, making sure there is adequate water in the bottom of the cooker.
10. Fasten the lid of the canner on tightly, so that no steam can escape around the edge of the lid.
11. Let steam escape from the pet cock for ten minutes, then close the pet cock.
12. As soon as the guage registers the pounds of pressure needed for your altitude, turn the heat down until you can maintain an even pressure for the time recommended. Follow the cooker manufacturer's directions carefully, to get good results and eliminate the danger of botulism.
13. At the end of the recommended cooking time, turn off the heat or slide the canner to a cool part of the stove. It will take thirty to forty-five minutes for the canner to cool down.
14. When the gauge returns to zero, open the pet cock slowly and wait until all the steam has escaped before opening the lid.
15. Remove lid from canner, tilting the canner away from your face to avoid being burned.
16. Using a jar lifter, remove the hot jars from the canner.
17. Put the jars in a draft-free place to cool. Do not cover them.
18. After twenty-four hours, check the jar lids to make sure they have all sealed. Refrigerate any jars that have not sealed and use the contents immediately.
19. Label the sealed jars, and store them in a cool, dry, dark place.

TABLE FOR PRESSURE CANNING CHILE

Altitude (feet)	Pressure (pounds)	Jar Size	Minutes to Process
2,000 to 4,000	12	1/2 pint	20
4,000 to 6,000	13	1 pint	25
6,000 to 8,000	14		
8,000 to 10,000	15		

GREEN CHILE SAUCE

5 or 6 green chiles, cut into cubes   1 tablespoon bacon drippings
1 medium onion, diced   or shortening
2 large tomatoes, cubed

1. Remove chile seeds, if desired, and chop coarsely.
2. Melt shortening in a skillet over medium heat.
3. Add chiles to shortening.
4. Add coarsely chopped tomatoes to chiles.
5. Fry all ingredients until soft, stirring constantly.
6. Add chopped onions and continue cooking until all ingredients are tender.
7. Add salt or garlic salt before serving, if desired.

Chile sauce is usually served with meats, beans, or stews. It is served more frequently in the summer and fall, when tomatoes and chiles are readily available.

RED CHILE SAUCE

[Approximately Two Cups]

24 medium-sized dried   garlic salt to taste
   red chile pods

1. Wash and dry chile pods.
2. Remove stems from pods, and also the seeds. The stems should be brittle and should break off easily. Shake out the dried seeds and save for planting.
3. Place chiles in a pot and cover with water. Cover pot and boil until tender.
4. Drain chiles and purée in blender with garlic salt.

Red chile sauce is used as a flavoring in other foods, as a substitute for catsup and mustard, or can be added to tamales. It keeps only a week or so in the refrigerator before molding, but can be stored up to a year in the freezer.

Should a chile sauce become too hot for comfort, stir in an egg to reduce the heat.

GREEN CHILE PASTE

[Approximately One Cup]

1. Roast and peel 6 fresh green chiles, according to the directions on page 49.
2. Remove and discard seeds (optional).
3. Put chiles in a blender and blend until they become a smooth purée.
4. Add plain or garlic salt to taste.

Chile paste is used in a number of ways: as a granish with stews, meat or bean dishes, or scrambled eggs; as a seasoning in other dishes; or as a spread for sandwiches. Tradition-conscious Hopi women mash the chiles into a paste consistency by hand, rather than using an electric blender.

Meat

Over an Open Fire

A meal without meat seems incomplete to most Indians. Northern Arizona's high country, with its vast acres of rich pine forests and clear streams, once supported abundant deer, antelope, elk, and other large game which Hopi men could kill and drag home for the village people to enjoy. Hunting is restricted by law now, but the men hunt in season and a big kill is still cause for celebration. I remember the excitement when a Polacca man caught a bear, while he and some of the young boys from the reservation were on a campout. The women of Polacca prepared the meat, and the people from the other villages on First Mesa joined in for a wonderful feast.

Although some Hopis raise cattle and sheep, and meat is readily available at trading posts on the reservation and supermarkets in nearby towns, hunting still means extra meat and a chance for the extended family to get together and socialize. When a large animal is killed, the aunts and other relatives gather for a feast, bringing someviki and other sumptuous things to go with the meat. Most of the meat is given away in this manner.

A Hopi feast is a "come, eat, and go" affair, so that as many guests as possible can be served. In times past, the meal was served on the floor, to make room for everyone. A large oil cloth or tablecloth was spread out, and the guests sat around it, eating out of common dishes with their fingers. Small game, such as rabbits and prairie dogs, are still plentiful in the desert areas, and experienced hunters catch them frequently—for feasts and other occasions. Such happy events as weddings, naming parties for the newborn, good harvests, and dance days always call for a feast.

Preparing Wild Game

Good meat comes from good shooting, with the best meat coming from healthy animals that appear alert and move quickly. Proper handling of game during the first six hours after the kill very much affects its quality and, because it is so important for food, Hopi hunters take great care to dress the meat cleanly and quickly in order to bring home a good piece.

Many of the rules for cooking domestic meat also apply to game. Here are a few tips for cooking both domestic and wild meat.

1. Use dry-heat methods, such as roasting, broiling, or pan broiling, for cooking tender cuts, and moist-heat methods for less tender. (In the popular Hopi Stew with Hominy, the meat is simmered for about one hour, the hominy is added along with the rock salt, and the stew is then simmered all night.

2. Tenderize meat by marinating it in lemon juice, tomato juice, or vinegar, or use commercial tenderizers.

3. Cut the long muscle fibers of very tough cuts by grinding, pounding, or scoring the meat.

4. Roast meats at low temperatures (300° to 325°F.) to reduce shrinkage and retain maximum nutrition and flavor.

BAKED PRAIRIE DOG (Tukya)

1 fresh-killed prairie dog
  per person
pepper

salt
nanakopsie, tuitsma,
  or other herb seasoning

1. Kill the prairie dogs and immediately singe the fur completely, to get rid of fleas. Scrape the carcass to remove any fur or ash and wash it well with clear water. Dress as you would a rabbit and leave whole.
2. Stuff body cavity with seasonings and salt and pepper.
3. Bake in a 350°F oven for three hours, or until tender.

When prairie dogs are in season and are prepared correctly, they are considered a delicacy. Fat prairie dogs have a milder flavor than lean ones.

HOW TO DRESS A RABBIT

1. Cut off the forelegs at the first joint.
2. Cut through the skin of the back legs.
3. Tie the back legs tightly together.
4. Hang the rabbit from a hook, upside down.
5. Pull the skin down over the thighs, then over the body, the head, and front legs, and discard.
6. Sever the head and discard.
7. Cut the back feet off at the heel joint.
8. With a sharp knife, slit the rabbit down the front (being careful not to cut too deep) and remove the entrails.
9. Wash the body cavity well with clear water.
10. Cut into serving pieces by severing the four legs at the joints, and cutting the body into three pieces. Or leave the rabbit whole for baking.

Although rabbits are hunted and eaten frequently by Hopis, they carry disease, as does other wild game including prairie dogs, and should only be killed and dressed by experienced hunters. Domestic rabbit is available in most states through breeders or markets and is much safer for the average housewife to handle.

FRIED RABBIT

1 rabbit, dressed and cut into serving-size pieces
1 quart water
3 tablespoons salt

salt and pepper to taste
1/2 cup flour
1/2 cup shortening
1/2 cup water

1. Dissolve 3 tablespoons salt in approximately one quart of water and soak the rabbit in it for one to two hours. (The water should cover the rabbit.)
2. Drain rabbit and pat dry.
3. Sprinkle rabbit pieces with salt and pepper and roll in flour.
4. Fry in hot shortening, 1/4-inch deep, as you would chicken. Turn pieces to brown on all sides.
5. Add 1/2 cup water, cover, and cook slowly for one and a half hours, or until tender.

Rabbit and other wild game can also be soaked in vinegar water, but Indians always use salt water. Domestic rabbit doesn't have to be soaked.

BAKED RABBIT

[Serves Six]

1 rabbit, dressed whole
2 to 3 tablespoons shortening or bacon drippings
1 cup coarsely ground cornmeal

1 teaspoon salt
1/4 cup nanakopsi
1/2 cup water

1. Rub rabbit with shortening and place in a greased casserole dish.
2. Mix salt with cornmeal and sprinkle over rabbit.
3. Sprinkle nanakopsie in the cavity.
4. Pour a 1/2 cup of water into the dish and cover dish with aluminum foil.
5. Bake in a 350°F oven for two hours or until tender.

Nanakopsie and tuitsma are herb seasonings that are grown and dried by the Hopi people themselves. They are not available commercially and there are no seasonings on the market that make good substitutes. Such herbs as sage and thyme can be used to make a tasty dish, but will give the rabbit a different flavor.

STUFFED RABBIT

[Serves Six]

1 rabbit, dressed whole
1 cup coarsely ground cornmeal
1 teaspoon salt
1/2 teaspoon pepper

3 tablespoons butter or margarine
1/2 cup chopped onion
1/4 cup chopped celery
1 1/2 cups water

1. Add salt and pepper to cornmeal.
2. Sauté onion and celery in butter or margarine and add to corn-meal.
3. Rinse rabbit and salt and pepper cavity lightly.
4. Put cornmeal mixture into cavity, but don't pack tightly.
5. Put stuffed rabbit in a baking dish, add 1½ cups of water, and cover.
6. Bake rabbit in 350°F oven for 1 1/2 hours, or until tender.

Hopi women use different methods to cook rabbit, to add variety to their menus.

RABBIT CORN BREAD (Quitaviki)

intestines from a freshly
   killed rabbit
1 teaspoon salt
1 cup coarsely ground
   white cornmeal

2 tablespoons butter
   or bacon drippings
1 cup warm water

Also:
20 corn husks

1. Wash the intestines well and grind in a meat grinder, using a fine blade.
2. Add salt and cornmeal to intestines and mix well.
3. Melt butter or bacon drippings in warm water and add to corn-meal mixture.
4. Put two rounded tablespoons of mixture into each corn husk, tying husks with two strips of corn husk as with tamales.
5. Place filled husks in a baking pan and bake in a 350°F oven for forty-five minutes.

This dish is served mainly by older people, who remember hard times and the importance of utilizing all nourishing parts of foods. The bread is served with fried, baked, or stewed rabbit, along with gravy or some other sauce.

DRIED RABBIT STEW WITH DUMPLINGS

[*Serves Six*]

1 dried rabbit
2 quarts water
1 tablespoon salt
1 medium onion, chopped

2 stalks celery, chopped
assorted other vegetables
dumplings (recipe below)

1. Undo forelegs from hind legs and wash rabbit thoroughly.
2. Place rabbit in a saucepan, cover with water, and simmer, covered, for thirty-five or forty minutes, or until tender.
3. Add salt, onion, celery, and other vegetables you like in a stew, and cook until tender.
4. Add dumplings, cover, and cook another ten minutes.

Dumplings

2 cups blue cornmeal
1 teaspoon salt
1 1/2 cups boiling water

1 tablespoon bacon drippings
or other shortening

1. Mix salt and cornmeal in a bowl.
2. Melt shortening in boiling water and add to dry ingredients, stirring to dissolve lumps.
3. When dough is cool enough to handle, roll into 1-inch balls, flatten with your hands, and drop into the boiling stew.

Drying meat is an older way of preserving it but is still practiced occasionally, especially by those who don't have refrigerators. Rabbit is dried by baking it in a 350°F oven for an hour, securing the back legs under the forelegs to form a circle, and hanging it in the open air for five days or more to dry thoroughly.

JERKY (TRADITIONAL METHOD)

1. Separate the meat from the bones and cut the individual muscles with a sharp knife, going round and round in a circular motion so you have long strips of meat. Strips should be no more than 1/4-inch thick. (When cut thicker, it takes the meat longer to dry and increases the chance of spoilage.)
2. Salt the meat strips or not, according to your preference.
3. Place meat in the sun for three or four days, depending on the thickness of the meat, to dry. Turn the meat twice a day to ensure even drying.

Jerky (dried meat) has been made from various meats including mutton, beef, venison, and even some rabbit. Indian women take great pride in the thinness and length of their jerky strips, and the thinness is certainly important for good preservation. Most of the women prefer to dry their meat in the hot sun, but a few have special drying racks on screened porches where they hang their strips. It takes meat longer to dry on these porches, however, than it does in the hot sun.

JERKY (OVEN DRIED)

1 1/2 pounds beef flank or other lean beef	1/2 teaspoon monosodium glutamate
1/4 cup soy sauce	1/2 teaspoon pepper
1 tablespoon liquid smoke	1 tablespoon worcestershire sauce
1/2 teaspoon garlic salt	

1. Partially freeze meat, then slice cross-grain into 1/8-inch slices.
2. Combine remaining ingredients to make a marinade.
3. Put meat in a bowl and pour marinade over it. Cover bowl and refrigerate meat overnight.
4. Place meat slices on a rack over a pan, such as a broiler pan, and bake in a 150°F oven, leaving door ajar, for six hours, or until the slices of beef are leathery dry. Turn slices every two hours.
5. Meat will keep one to two days at room temperature and up to two weeks in a covered container in the refrigerator.

Oven dried jerky is very tasty and is usually gobbled up before it has time to spoil.

WAYS TO USE JERKY

1. Cover jerky with water and simmer until tender. Then pound it in a mortar and pestle, or chop in a blender, and add to cornmeal gravy.
2. Roast and serve with chile and tortillas.
3. Use in tamales.
4. Make hash.
5. Add to stews.
6. Boil bite-size pieces and drop in dumplings.
7. Cook and pound jerky and fry with chile for breakfast.
8. Cut dried meat into serving pieces and fry in a small amount of shortening. Add 2 cups of water and bring to a boil. Crack eggs and drop into the skillet with meat. Cover and let stand until eggs set.
9. Cut into four-inch strips, and broil until crisp; it burns easily, so check often.

HOMINY STEW

[*Serves Ten*]

2 pounds mutton or beef backbones, cut into 1-inch serving sizes
water

10 cups hominy (see page 35) (fresh, dried, or frozen)
1 tablespoon salt

1. Put meat in a large pot, cover with water, and stir in salt.
2. Cover pot and simmer meat for about one hour, and then add hominy.
3. Continue cooking, in covered pot, until hominy becomes soft, usually overnight.

Mrs. Margaret Calnimptewa
Hotevilla, Arizona

TAMALES

[Two Dozen]

Dough

2 cups finely ground cornmeal
1/2 teaspoon salt

1 1/2 cups meat broth
(saved from meat filling below)

Also:
2 dozen fresh corn husks
  (or dried corn husks that have
  been soaked in water until
  they are limber)

1. Mix together the cornmeal, salt, and meat broth.
2. Stretch a prepared corn husk as flat as possible and spread a tablespoon of dough from the center of the husk downward, leaving 1 1/2-inch margins at the sides and bottom. If dough does not spread easily, dip fingers in water and pat dough to spread.
3. Spread a tablespoon of meat mixture over the dough, but not quite to the edges of it.
4. Fold the right and left sides of the corn husk over the filling. Then fold the pointed end of the husk up to the middle of the tamale.
5. Tie a corn husk string around the middle of the tamale and another around the thicker end of the corn husk, to keep the filling in.
6. Stand the tamales, folded ends down, in a large pot.
7. Fill the bottom of the pot (or steamer) with three inches of water. Cover pot and steam tamales for two hours over medium heat.

Meat Filling for Tamales

1 1/2 pounds ground beef or lamb
2/3 pound ground pork
2 teaspoons salt
1 teaspoon garlic powder

1/4 cup chile powder
1/2 cup coarsely ground cornmeal
2 cups water

1. Brown meats in a saucepan or deep frying pan. (Add shortening if pork doesn't provide enough fat to prevent meat from sticking.)
2. Stir in salt and other seasonings.
3. Add the remaining ingredients, cover, and simmer gently for forty-five minutes. Stir mixture occasionally and taste for seasoning. Add more chile or other seasoning if necessary.
4. Drain the meat mixture, saving the liquid for the dough. If necessary, add more water to meat broth to make 1 1/2 cups.

VENISON, ANTELOPE, OR ELK SWISS STEAK

[Serves Eight to Ten]

2 pounds round steak,
   1/2-inch thick
1/2 cup flour
1 teaspoon salt
1 teaspoon pepper

2 to 3 tablespoons shortening
1 cup canned tomatoes
3 large onions, chopped
1 cup water

1. Cut meat into serving-size pieces.
2. Mix flour, salt, and pepper and dredge meat with mixture.
3. Brown both sides of meat in hot shortening.
4. Put browned meat in a casserole, add other ingredients, cover, bake in a 350°F oven for one and a half to two hours, or until meat is tender. (Or cover and cook over a low flame on top of the stove.)
5. Remove meat to a platter and thicken gravy with flour or corn starch. Pour gravy over meat to serve.

This is a good way to use the less tender cuts of wild game. Other ways to use game are to grind it for burgers, or to make mincemeat (an Anglo influence), hash, tamales, meat pies, or jerky.

VENISON ROAST

2 pounds boneless venison roast
2/3 cup cooking oil
   (or bacon drippings)

1 teaspoon salt
1 onion, chopped fine
3 slices bacon

1. Make a marinade of oil, salt, and onion.
2. Put meat in a large bowl and pour marinade over it. Cover bowl and refrigerate meat overnight.
3. Transfer meat to a baking pan and lay the bacon slices over it.
4. Cover the baking pan and roast meat in a 325°F oven for twenty minutes per pound, or until done. Baste occasionally.

VENISON AND VEGETABLE STEW

2 pounds venison, cut into 1-inch cubes	3 tablespoons cooking oil (or bacon drippings)
1/2 cup flour	1 quart water
1 onion, chopped fine	2 tablespoons dried nanakopsie
1 cup diced celery	3 carrots, sliced
2 tablespoons diced green chile	2 potatoes, diced

1. Roll meat in flour, brown in hot oil, and transfer to a cooking kettle.
2. Sauté onion, celery, and chile in hot oil for two minutes and add to meat in kettle.
3. Rinse frying pan with 1 quart of water and pour over the meat and vegetables.
4. Stir in nanakopsie.
5. Cover pot and simmer one to two hours, or until meat is almost tender.
6. Add carrots and potatoes to stew and continue to cook until the potatoes are done.

Turnips or other vegetables in season can be added to the stew also.

VENISON CHILE

[Serves Six]

1/2 cup beef suet	2 tablespoons chile powder (or more, according to taste)
2 pounds ground venison	1 teaspoon paprika
1 medium onion, chopped	1 quart water
2 cloves garlic, minced	
1 tablespoon salt	

1. Melt suet in heavy kettle.
2. Add meat to suet and brown.
3. Add onion and seasonings.
4. Pour in water to cover meat.
5. Cover kettle and simmer meat for four to five hours, stirring occasionally and adding extra water as needed.
6. Serve with tortillas or fried bread and a green salad.

VENISON HASH

[Serves Six]

3 tablespoons shortening
1 pound ground venison
1 medium onion, chopped
4 stalks celery, finely chopped

3 medium potatoes, diced
1 teaspoon salt
1 teaspoon pepper
1 cup water

1. Heat shortening in a large skillet.
2. Add meat, onion, celery, and potatoes, stirring to coat the vegetables with oil.
3. Stir in salt and pepper.
4. Add 1 cup water, cover skillet, and simmer meat and vegetables for one and a half hours, stirring occasionally to prevent burning.

Leftover roast or steak can also be cubed and used in hash.

WHOLE WHEAT STEW

3 cups whole wheat
1 pound stew meat
1/4 cup chopped onions

1 tablespoon salt
water

1. Wash whole wheat well and cover with lukewarm water. Soak wheat overnight to soften.
2. Drain wheat and grind on stone to remove hulls.
3. Put hulled wheat in a large cooking pot and cover with water.
4. Add meat, onions, and salt to whole wheat.
5. Cover stew and simmer for three hours, or until wheat has softened and meat is tender. Stir occasionally and add water as needed.
6. Serve with your favorite bread and a green salad.

Hulled whole wheat can be purchased from grist mills and some specialty stores.

FRESH CORN STEW

[Serves Four]

1 cup ground meat
1 tablespoon shortening
salt and pepper to taste
2 cups fresh green corn,
    cut from cob

1 cup summer squash, cubed
2 cups water (approximately)
·1 tablespoon whole wheat flour
    or cornmeal

1. Brown meat in shortening and stir in salt and pepper.
2. Add vegetables to meat and cover with water.
3. Cover stew and simmer for thirty minutes, or until vegetables are almost tender.
4. Stir 2 tablespoons of water into flour until smooth and add to stew.
5. Simmer five more minutes, stirring to prevent scorching.

Other vegetables with similar cooking times can be added also. Or blue corn dumplings can be dropped on top of the stew.

SCORCHED CORN STEW (Twoitsie)

[Serves Ten]

2 cups dried beans
3 ears last year's corn
1 tablespoon salt

4 pounds meat
    (beef, mutton, or rabbit)
water

1. Wash and sort beans, put in a large kettle, add water to cover, and simmer for an hour or so.
2. Clean corn with a vegetable brush, then wipe with a damp cloth.
3. Hold ears of corn over a low flame or electric burner on your stove until they brown, turning ears so that all kernels get scorched.
4. Scrape burned edges from the cobs and shell corn.
5. Cut meat into serving-size pieces and add meat and corn to beans.
6. Stir in salt.
7. Cover stew and simmer for three hours, or until beans and corn are tender. Stir occasionally and add water if needed.
8. Serve with bread and chile.

Large quantities of corn are browned, or scorched, over live coals out-of-doors.

MEAT TURNOVERS

Meat Filling

1 1/2 pounds ground beef or lamb   8 tablespoons powdered chile
1 teaspoon salt   1 medium onion, chopped fine
garlic powder to taste   1 cup tomatoes

1. Brown meat well in a small saucepan or frying pan.
2. Add seasonings and onion, stirring well.
3. Add tomatoes and cover and simmer meat for one hour, stirring frequently to keep from burning. (Meat should be almost dry.)

Yeast Dough for Turnovers

1 package dry yeast   1/2 teaspoon salt
  (or 1 cake of yeast)   2 tablespoons sugar
1 1/2 cups water   4 tablespoons powdered milk
3 tablespoons shortening   3 cups flour (approximately)

1. Dissolve yeast in 1/4 cup warm water.
2. In large mixing bowl, stir together the rest of the water (1 1/4 cups), shortening, salt, sugar, and powdered milk.
3. Add yeast to above ingredients and enough flour to make a medium-stiff dough. Do not let dough rise.
4. Roll dough 1/8-inch thick and cut into 2 1/2-inch circles with a biscuit cutter or floured glass.
5. Put 1 1/2 tablespoons of meat filling in the center of each circle.
6. Fold dough on top of filling, pinching edges together.
7. Place turnovers on a cookie sheet, folded edges down, and let rest for eight minutes.
8. Bake turnovers in a 425°F oven for fifteen to twenty minutes, or until brown.

Biscuit Dough for Turnovers

2 cups sifted all-purpose flour
4 teaspoons baking powder
1/2 teaspoon salt
1/2 teaspoon cream of tartar
2 teaspoons sugar

1/2 cup shortening
2/3 cup milk (or 3 tablespoons
    powdered milk and
    2/3 cup water)

1. Sift together flour, salt, baking powder, sugar, cream of tartar, and powdered milk.
2. Cut in shortening until mixture resembles coarse crumbs.
3. Add milk all at once (or water if powdered milk is used), stirring only until dough sticks together.
4. Flour a breadboard lightly and gently knead dough on board for thirty seconds.
5. Divide dough into 14 balls and roll each ball into 1/4-inch thick squares or circles.
6. Put a heaping tablespoon of meat filling on each piece of dough and fold edges of dough over filling, pinching edges together to seal.
7. Place turnovers, folded edges down, on lightly greased pan and bake at 425°F for fifteen to twenty minutes, or until brown.

CHILE ROLLS

Filling

1 pound ground meat
1 medium onion, chopped fine
1 teaspoon salt

1/2 teaspoon garlic powder
2 tablespoons chile powder

1. Brown meat in a small saucepan or frying pan.
2. Add onion and other seasonings and continue to cook until meat is almost dry. Stir constantly to keep meat from burning.
3. Set aside until you have made the dough for the rolls.

Dough

2 cups sifted all-purpose flour
1/2 teaspoon salt
3 teaspoons baking powder
3 tablespoons dry milk powder

1/4 cup shortening
2/3 cup warm water or
 2/3 cup whole milk

1. Sift dry ingredients into a mixing bowl (including powdered milk, if using).
2. Cut shortening into dry ingredients until it is the size of peas.
3. Add water (or fresh milk) to make a soft dough.
4. Roll dough 1/2-inch thick and cut into 4-inch circles.
5. Fill each circle with 2 tablespoons of meat filling, and fold dough over filling and seal edges.
6. Bake rolls on a biscuit pan or cookie sheet, edges down, in a 400°F oven for twenty minutes, or until golden brown.

Chile rolls are good served with vegetables or a salad for a main meal. Or they are handy to take on picnics or to bake sales.

PAN FRIED LAMB

[Serves Eight]

2 pounds lamb
salt and pepper to taste

1/2 cup flour
1/2 cup shortening

1. Cut meat into serving pieces.
2. Salt and pepper meat and roll in flour.
3. Fry in hot shortening as you would chicken, turning to cook evenly.
4. Serve with tortillas, chili paste, and any vegetables that are in season.

When twin lambs are born to a ewe, one is usually butchered for the table to spare the mother; the other is saved for the herd.

LAMB STEW WITH NANAKOPSIE

[Serves Eight]

2 pounds young lamb,
    cut into serving pieces
salt and pepper to taste
water

2 bunches fresh nanakopsie
    (or 2 tablespoons
    dried nanakopsie)

1. Put meat into a stew pot and cover with water.
2. Add nanakopsie and salt and pepper.
3. Cover pot and simmer meat for two hours or until tender.
4. Serve with Hopi Finger Bread and a chile sauce.

Greens
and Fruits

Wild Harvest

Edible wild greens and fruits have always been a part of the Hopi diet. A few plants grow on the rocky terrain of the mesas themselves, but even more grow in the richer soil of the valleys below. Although modern homemakers often use the more convenient canned or frozen vegetables, some still gather the succulent wild greens when they appear in the spring and summer.

Gathering greens is usually a social event, when families or groups of friends get together to go out and pick. But not always. A friend and I were collecting money for a charitable cause recently, when we spotted a cluster of plants that make particularly good tea. It was just too good an opportunity to pass up, and we stopped by the side of the road and gathered up as much as we could carry.

Some of the greens are so tender and sweet, they can be eaten raw. Others are good when steamed lightly. Still others, especially those used to make the various teas, are dried and stored. A number of plants are also dried for seasonings, like nanakopsie and tuitsma.

The Indians burn some plant species and use the ashes to color foods such as cornbreads. These so-called culinary ashes add more than decoration, however, as they are rich in essential minerals including calcium, magnesium, phosphorus, and potassium. Hopis prefer ashes from the four-winged saltbush, as it is very alkaline and, when used correctly, lends a distinct blue color to foods.

Wild greens start putting up shoots as early as March and some continue to produce as late as August and September. The greens must be picked when young and tender, because the leaves and stems of most edible wild plants become tough and woody as they mature. No one should undertake to gather and eat unfamiliar plants, however, as many tempting leaves and berries are actually very poisonous. The Hopi people have been gathering plants and herbs for many centuries and learn to recognize the edible ones at an early age. They also learn to leave a few plants to go to seed, so that there will be more greens next year.

HOW TO DRY GREENS

1. Clean and sort greens, removing any tough leaves, stems, or foreign matter such as grass and burrs.
2. Wash greens in cool running water to remove sand and dirt.
3. Spread leaves on drying racks or clean cloths and put in the shade to dry. (Although leaves dry faster in the sun, this process bleaches the green from the plants.)
4. Turn leaves daily to ensure even drying.
5. String or bundle dry leaves or store in sacks or jars, as you desire.

Things do not have to be complicated to be good. Drying greens is a simple way of preserving them, one that has been practiced by the Indians for many generations.

DRIED SALT GREENS (Ongatoki)

4 cups dried salt greens   5 cups water

1. Wash greens well, until all sand is removed.
2. Pick leaves from stems, if stems are too brittle to become tender with cooking.
3. Cover greens with water and bring to a boil.
4. Cover and simmer for fifteen minutes, or until greens become tender.
5. Drain greens and season with bacon drippings or butter.

Salt greens are small plants that grow close to the ground, mainly in clay soils in the valley below the mesas. The leaves are thicker than the leaves of most plants and have a decidedly salty taste, hence their name. Although the Hopi people weren't eating as many wild greens in the 1970s as in earlier times, they did gather and eat salt greens.

NATIVE GREENS WITH CORNMEAL DUMPLINGS

[*Serves Six*]

2 cups blue cornmeal
1 teaspoon salt
1/4 cup bacon drippings
   or cooking oil

11 cups boiling water
4 cups cooked greens
   (frozen, dried or canned)
1 cup cooked meat, diced

1. In a large pot, bring 11 cups of water to a rolling boil. (This will be enough water for the broth and the dumplings.)
2. Measure blue cornmeal into a medium-sized mixing bowl.
3. Add salt and drippings to cornmeal.
4. Gradually add 2 2/3 cups boiling water to the cornmeal mixture and mix well with a wooden spoon. (Boiling water is necessary for the dumplings to retain their shape.)
5. Set dough aside to cool.
6. Add cooked greens to the remaining boiling water.
7. Add diced meat to the greens.
8. When the dumpling dough becomes cool enough to handle, knead it until it stays together (about 4 minutes).
9. Roll dough into half-inch balls, and flatten them into 1/8-inch thick dumplings.
10. Drop dumplings into boiling greens.
11. Cover and simmer for 30 minutes. Serve warm.

Any edible greens can be used in this recipe.

DANDELION GREENS

1. Gather greens early in the spring when the leaves are young and tender, and before the plants start to bloom. Once the dandelion flowers appear, the leaves begin to turn bitter.
2. Cut the leaves off at the root stalk.
3. Rinse the greens in cool, running water to remove sand and grit.
4. Cook as you would spinach or swiss chard.

Dandelion greens are delicious when picked early and are reputed to be a good source of iron, calcium, potassium, and vitamins C and A.

KWAAKWI SOMEVIKI

1 cup kwaakwi   1/2 cup boiling water
1 cup white corn flour   1 quart water

Also:
2 dozen fresh corn husks
  (or dried husks that have been
  soaked in water)

1. Mix kwaakwi and corn flour.
2. Stir in 1/2 cup boiling water.
3. Put a tablespoon of batter in each corn husk, fold husks around batter, and tie husks in two places with strips of corn husk or yucca.
4. Bring 1 quart of water to a rolling boil.
5. Drop tied husks in water, cover, and simmer for thirty minutes. Cool rolls before serving.

Kwaakwi is a native grass seed, resembling wheat, that grows in the valley below the mesas. The tassles are either cut and thrashed for the seed, or they are simply pulled through the fingers and the seeds are collected in the hands. In the past, when the Hopis kept more sheep, the men and boys would gather the seed while they herded. Depending on the amount of moisture, there was usually plenty for both the Indians and their animals, who liked it also.

RUSSIAN THISTLE

1. Gather very young plants and wash well.
2. Put into prepared corn husks, add seasonings, and fold husks around greens as in cooking tamales.
3. Put husks in a dutch oven or other cooking kettle, add 2 cups of water, cover oven, and simmer greens for thirty minutes, or until tender.
4. Greens can also be steamed, as in cooking spinach.

Russian thistle is a prevalent weed that grows throughout the spring and summer and is a menace to gardeners and farmers alike. Very young plants are tender and tasty, but the leaves quickly become tough, even too tough for sheep to eat. Very few, if any, Hopis cook Russian thistle anymore; they leave it for the sheep and cattle to eat.

PIT-BAKED GREENS

Often, when a family was working in the fields, fresh greens, such as the delicately flavored western tansy mustard greens (kwivi), were gathered and baked in a small pit. The pit was dug about ten inches deep and twelve inches square and was lined with flat stones. A fire was built in the pit, and a fresh layer of stones was placed over the hot coals. When these stones were hot, a layers of greens four inches high or more was put in. The pit was then covered with a flat stone, and the edges were sealed with mud plaster to seal in the steam that was generated from the moisture in the plants. When the plants had steamed for thirty minutes, the plaster and stone were carefully removed, and the cooked greens were transferred to a bowl for a delicious and healthful out-of-doors meal.

Various tender greens can also be steamed in a pot on the stove. Wild greens should be washed and picked over well, to remove sand and tough stems and leaves, before being dropped in the pot. The pot is then covered and the greens are steamed for twenty to twenty-five minutes, or until tender, in the moisture that clung to them while they were being washed.

BAKED SQUASH BLOSSOMS (Sipongviki)

12 large squash blossoms   3 tablespoons bacon drippings
 1 cup blue cornmeal   or shortening
1/2 teaspoon salt   3/4 cup water (approximately)

1. Early in the morning before the blossoms close, cut blossoms with a sharp knife.
2. Rinse the blossoms gently and drain.
3. Mix cornmeal, salt and shortening in a mixing bowl.
4. Slowly add water, while stirring, to make a thick dough that you can handle with your fingers.
5. Gently stuff the blossoms with a teaspoon of dough each.
6. Fold blossom edges over the dough, to keep dough from falling out while baking.
7. Place blossoms stem up on a lightly greased pan.
8. Bake in a 300°F oven for twenty minutes.

Chopped green chiles may be added to dough.

FRIED NANHA

1. Gather nanha, or corn smut, from infected ears when it is tender and moist.
2. Wash it carefully to remove sand and corn silks.
3. Put it in a saucepan and cover with water.
4. Cover pan and simmer nanha for ten minutes.
5. Drain nanha and sauté it in butter or margarine until it is lightly browned and crisp.
6. Serve hot.

Corn smut is a common fungus, akin to mushrooms, that grows on corn. Older Hopis considered it a real delicacy but few young Hopis have eaten it. The children do play with it out in the corn fields, however, by chasing one another and smearing it on those who get caught. This game has become a traditional part of the baking sweet corn activities. After the sweet corn has been picked and loaded on the trucks, the many relatives and friends who have been asked to help are ready to play. Adults and children alike join in the chasing and smearing fun, with the boys usually sided against the girls.

CULINARY ASHES

Culinary ashes are made by burning certain bushes or trees until they crumble into ash. Creeks and Seminoles use hickory, and Navajos use primarily juniper branches. Hopis may use various materials, such as spent bean vines and pods or corn cobs, but Hopi women prefer ashes made from green plants, since they are more alkaline. They especially prize the ash from the four-winged saltbush (*Atriplex canescens*). This bush, which is also called suwvi or chamisa, can be found in abundance in the desert areas of the Hopi reservation. It grows in clumps similar to sagebrush and produces a very hard wood. When burned, green chamisa bushes yield culinary ashes high in mineral content. Dr. Doris Calloway, a nutritionist at the University of California at Berkeley, has done tests which show that old plants have only a fraction of the potassium, magnesium, and sodium found in ash made from green plants.

The Hopi practice of adding culinary ashes to corn dishes therefore raises the already substantial mineral content of these foods. In addition to increasing nutritional value, chamisa ashes enhance the color in blue corn products. When one is using blue cornmeal for any dish, the meal will turn pink when hot water is added, so Hopi women mix chamisa ashes with water to make an "ash broth" which is then strained and added to cornmeal mixtures in measured amounts. The high alkaline content of the chamisa ashes create a distinctly blue-green color, which holds a religious significance for the Hopis.

Care must be taken when chopping down the bushes, as snakes, including rattlers, seek the relative cool of the shade of the bush. A hoe or shovel is used to clear and clean off an area approximately six feet square, where the cut bushes are stacked after removing any dried tumbleweeds that might be caught in the branches. The chamisa is piled about five feet high, and the fire is started. We use a pitchfork to move branches into the center of the fire to make sure that all is completely burned to ashes. When the fire has burned out and cooled down, the ashes are put into buckets or tubs, and then sifted to remove any twigs or sticks not burned. Chamisa ashes should be stored in a container with a tightly fitting lid.

The saltbush was also used as a laundry agent in times past. The women would wet the bush, then rub it between their hands to make suds for washing clothes.

YUCCA PIE

1/2 cup sugar
1/4 teaspoon ground cloves
3 tablespoons butter
1/4 cup heavy cream

1/2 teaspoon cinnamon
3 cups chopped uncooked yucca
  fruit
pastry for 2-crust pie

1. Line pie plate with pastry.
2. In a bowl, mix the fruit with rest of ingredients.
3. Pour fruit mixture into pie shell and top with pastry. Pierce pastry with a fork to allow steam to escape.
4. Bake at 375°F for thirty minutes.

The Indians use the yucca plant in many ways, so much so that it is becoming scarce. Besides the fruit, young yucca leaves are used to make baskets. The tender new shoots are pulled from the middle of the plant in early spring and are dried until they become white in color and of a texture suitable for weaving baskets. The more mature yucca leaves are pulled into thin strips, to make strings for tying tamales and other dishes cooked in corn husks.

DRIED YUCCA FRUIT

1. Cut fruit into long, thin strips.
2. Lay strips in the sunshine to dry. Turn daily to ensure thorough drying.
3. Store strips in covered containers for later use.

BOILED YUCCA FRUIT

1. Wash fruit and cut it up into a pot.
2. Cover fruit with water and simmer, covered, for one to three hours, depending on freshness of fruit.
3. Remove lid and continue cooking until fruit has boiled down into a jam-like consistency. Stir frequently to prevent scorching.
4. Serve with someviki or sliced bread.

BAKED YUCCA FRUIT

1. Gather fruit from the tall stalks of the yucca plant in July and August when it has fully ripened.
2. Wash the fruit thoroughly but do not peel.
3. Bake the fruit in a slow oven (300°F) for two and a half hours, or until tender. The cooked fruit should have the consistency of applesauce.

Before the Spaniards and others brought peaches, apples, apricots, and other fruits into Arizona, the yucca and a few berries were the only sweet fruits the Hopis had. The yucca fruit is knocked off the tall plants with sticks, but it must be ripe to fall easily. The fruit is large and is usually baked in earth ovens by the Hopis.

PRICKLY PEAR PADS

1. Gather tender thick pads from the prickly pear cactus plant in April or early May. Use tongs to remove the pads, or cut them off with a shovel.
2. Singe the pads to remove the hair-like thorns, or remove them carefully with a paring knife.
3. Put pads in a large saucepan and cover with water. (Use water from boiled baked sweet corn if you have it available, or add a stem or two of baked sweet corn to the water.)
4. Cover pot and boil pads for twenty to thirty minutes, or until tender.
5. Drain water from pads, to remove stickers, and chop or dice pads, one at a time, on a cutting board. Rinse the board after each pad.
6. Put the chopped fruit into another saucepan and simmer, stirring frequently to keep fruit from scorching, until pads have become a thick, mucilaginous juice.
7. Serve as a dip with Hopi Finger Bread.

Although many older Hopis remember eating prickly pear dishes when they were young, very few gathered the fruit in the 1970s. In the past, the fruit was also dried and ground, and used as a sweetener in many traditional dishes such as someviki.

WOLFBERRY JAM

1. Gather berries in early summer when they are large and juicy.
2. Sort and wash berries and put them in a pot with just enough water to cover them.
3. Simmer berries, covered, for one hour, then drain off the water.
4. Grind the berries in a meat grinder to make a jam-like consistency.
5. Add 1 cup of potato clay to the berries.
6. Serve as jam with fresh piki.

Wolfberries, or Kevepsi in Hopi, grow on small bushes in desert areas. They are orange to red when ripe and sweet enough to eat right off the bush.

Potato clay is a very fine clay found at the foot of the mesas. It is mixed with water to the consistency of thick cream and then used as a dip to neutralize the acid in wild potatoes or to add flavor and minerals to foods.

SUVIPSI "LEMONADE"

1. Gather ripe berries from the suvipsi, or squaw bush, plant.
2. Add water to berries, bring to a boil, and allow mixture to steep. Mash berries slightly, if desired.
3. Pour water off berries and add sugar or honey and ice cubes. Discard berries.

Squaw bushes grow readily on the mesas, in crevices and other shady, rocky areas. The berries ripen in summer and are small, somewhat flat in shape, and deep red in color. The berries are extremely sour, even when ripe, but make a refreshing hot or cold drink.

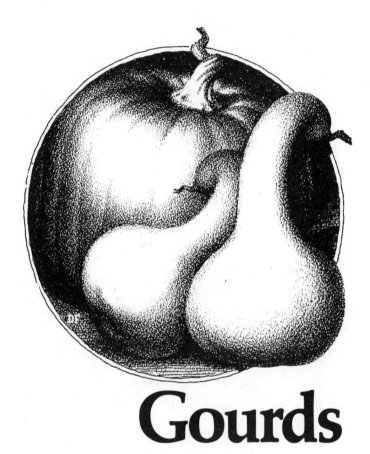

Gourds

Vine-grown Goodness

For centuries the Hopis have put many varieties of the gourd family to good use. In addition to creating nourishing meals from edible gourds, they utilize the hard shells of small ornamental gourds for water dippers, spoons, small bowls, and even baby rattles.

Pumpkins and squashes are important vegetables in the Hopi diet. Most of the types grown on the Hopi Reservation are hard-shelled varieties that ripen on the vine in early fall but can be stored until as late as the following February or March. Softer-shelled varieties are also grown but don't keep as well, and the flesh is cut into thin strips and dried for winter use. One of the oldest and most popular Hopi squashes is the green-striped cushaw, which is grown each year from seeds of earlier crops. The men plant new varieties also, from seeds ordered from catalogs or purchased from local stores.

Indians don't customarily end meals with sweet desserts, but serve fruit and puddings with the main course. Younger Hopis, influenced by Anglo ways, do serve ice cream or cake, and even turn pumpkins and squashes into pies and other delicacies, as the Anglos do.

USES FOR THE STRIPED CUSHAW

1. Boil or bake the meat of the squash.
2. Remove the rind and cut the flesh into spirals. Dry for winter use.
3. Roast the seeds for eating.
4. Cut the hard shell in half horizontally and clean and dry the lower half for a container. (Children use these to carry parched corn.)

The striped cushaw has been excavated in a number of Indian sites in the Southwest. It is still commonly cultivated.

SQUASH AND FRESH CORN CASSEROLE

8 ears fresh corn
10 small, tender, green summer
   squash (about 2 pounds)
2 tablespoons shortening
1 medium onion, chopped
1 clove garlic, minced
   (or 1/2 teaspoon
   powdered garlic)

2 green chile peppers, chopped
2 large tomatoes, chopped
   (or 1/2 cup canned tomatoes)
2 cups fresh lima beans
2 cups green beans, sliced
1 teaspoon salt
black pepper to taste
1 cup water

1. Wash corn and cut from cobs.
2. Wash and cube squash.
3. Heat shortening in a large kettle and add all vegetables except corn. Sauté until vegetables are clear, stirring constantly.
4. Add water and simmer until beans are done, stirring frequently to prevent scorching.
5. Add corn and cook ten minutes longer.
6. Serve as a vegetable or a main dish.

FRESH PUMPKIN PIE

1 1/3 cups fresh pumpkin puree
2 eggs, slightly beaten
2 cups evaporated milk
3/4 cup brown sugar
1 teaspoon salt

1 1/2 teaspoons cinnamon
1 1/2 teaspoons ginger
1/4 teaspoon cloves
pastry for one-crust pie

1. Line pie plate with pastry.
2. Stir eggs and milk into pumpkin. Add sugar, salt, and spices and mix well.
3. Pour pumpkin mixture into pastry and bake at 450°F for ten minutes, then reduce heat to 350°F and bake for an additional thirty minutes, or until a knife inserted in the center comes out clean.

Pumpkin Puree

1. Cut pumpkin in half and remove seeds.
2. Peel pumpkin and cut into 1-inch cubes.
3. Put cubes into a saucepan and add 1/2 to 1 cup of water (only enough to keep pumpkin from burning).
4. Cover saucepan and simmer pumpkin, stirring often, until it becomes thick and mushy.
5. Mash pumpkin or whirl in a blender to purée.

Yellow squash can be substituted for pumpkin in this recipe.

BAKED PUMPKIN

1 ripe pumpkin   2 tablespoons butter
3 to 4 tablespoons sugar

1. Wash pumpkin, remove seeds, and cut into serving-size pieces.
2. Put pumpkin in a baking dish, flesh side up, and pierce flesh with a fork.
3. Cover with aluminum foil and bake in a 350°F oven for forty-five minutes, or until tender.
4. Remove foil and sprinkle pumpkin with sugar and butter. Cover and bake for an additional fifteen minutes. (More or less sugar and butter can be added according to taste and the size of the pumpkin.)

The Indians usually bake pumpkins and squash rather than fry them, and serve them as vegetables rather than desserts.

SUN CHOKES

1 pound sun chokes   salt and pepper to taste
¼ cup bacon drippings

1. Scrub sun chokes well to get the sand out of the many little crevices.
2. Peel chokes and cut them into 1/8-inch thick slices.
3. Heat bacon drippings and fry slices in a covered skillet until tender.
4. Serve in place of potatoes.

Sun chokes, or Jerusalem artichokes, are not true gourds, but are grown in many gardens on the Hopi Reservation, and are utilized in the diet in much the same way that gourds are. Sun chokes are left in the ground during the winter months and are dug as needed. In the spring, they reemerge as fresh plants without further cultivation.

Sun chokes are also good when rubbed with oil or wrapped in aluminum foil and baked, like potatoes, or even when eaten raw.

Beverages

Quenching Desert Thirst

The climate of northern Arizona's desert mesas is extremely dry. Because of this low humidity, the Hopi people have conditioned themselves to drink little water. In earlier times, women and young girls would gather at a spring before dawn and stand in line until each had filled her jug. Modern reservation dwellers have pickup trucks and haul water in cans from windmills—but some still have to travel as far as ten or twelve miles to get it. Water is not wasted in this arid area, and children are never encouraged to play in it. In fact, children of earlier generations were trained to return to their own homes when they wanted a drink, so they wouldn't deplete another family's supply of water.

Herb teas and fruit-based drinks, such as those described in this book, were the main beverages of earlier Hopis, and some still drink Indian teas regularly. But Anglo drinks such as Kool-Aid and Coca Cola are stocked by even remote reservation stores and have become very popular with adults as well as children. Commercial teas and coffees, prepared in the ways that most Anglos prepare them, are also popular, especially at mealtime.

Although some cattle is raised on the reservation, there are no milk cows or goats. Actually very little fresh milk is used by reservation homemakers, due to the lack of refrigeration. Children get milk at school, of course, but otherwise drink the traditional beverages or modern soft drinks that their parents enjoy.

HOHOISE TEA

1 pinch dried hohoise leaves, flowers, and stems
1 1/2 cups water

1. Boil the hohoise in water until the tea becomes dark orange in color.
2. Strain tea into cups and serve at once.

Hohoise is a perennial that grows in woodlands and on dry hills, in deep canyons and on top of mesas, from Mexico to Wyoming. It grows along the roadsides on the Hopi reservation and in Hopi fields and gardens. The leaves are dried on a rack in the sun, or placed in a 300°F oven for twenty minutes, or until dry.

HOPI TEA (Sita)

1 small pinch dried thelesperma leaves
1 1/2 cups water

Boil the thelesperma leaves in the water until the desired strength is reached. Serve hot.

Wild thelesperma leaves are gathered in the spring and the leaves and small stems of the plant are dried for tea.

Mrs. Glendora Tenakhongva
Hotevilla, Arizona

DRIED PEACH AND CORNMEAL DRINK (Sepal Tocie)

1/2 cup dried peaches
  (see page 104)
1 cup unsalted parched corn

1/2 cup water
additional water as needed

1. Grind peaches and parched corn together.
2. Add 1/2 cup water to the peaches and corn and stir until lumps are dissolved.
3. Add additional water to make a beverage of thin, cream-like consistency.
4. Serve cold instead of soft drinks.

HOPI MILK DRINK

1 cup powdered milk
1 cup finely ground blue
  cornmeal

5 3/4 cups warm water
3/4 cup cool water

1. Put powdered milk in a saucepan and add 3/4 cup of warm water, stirring until milk is smooth.
2. Add the remaining warm water and place saucepan in a double boiler or over low heat.
3. Cook slowly for ten minutes, stirring to prevent scorching.
4. In a small bowl, mix the cornmeal with 3/4 cup of cool water, stirring to remove lumps.
5. Add cornmeal mixture to the simmering milk, stirring until well mixed.
6. Continue to cook for five more minutes, stirring often.
7. Add sugar or a dash of salt to taste.

This is a tasty drink that has little or no sugar, according to taste, and a lot of vitamins and minerals. It is adapted from an old recipe and is used frequently by modern Hopis, especially as a bedtime drink or instead of cocoa.

CORNMEAL SAUCE (Wutaka)

[Serves One]

1/2 cup finely ground blue cornmeal

2 rounded teaspoons chamisa ash
3/4 cup boiling water

1. Mix together the chamisa ash with 3 tablespoons of boiling water, and set aside.
2. Put the cornmeal into a saucepan and add the rest of the boiling water, stirring to prevent lumps from forming.
3. Strain the ash water through cheesecloth or a fine-mesh strainer into the cornmeal mixture, a little at a time, until the color becomes blue-green.
4. Cook over low heat for approximately ten minutes, until mixture thickens. Stir to prevent scorching.
5. Serve hot with piki or roasted piki for a light meal.

This dish is often requested by elderly Hopis and the very ill.

Between Meals

The Occasional Treat

Happiness to an Indian child is a pocket full of puffed parched corn and a few friends to share it with. He can play with it, trade it to other children, or nibble on it and not worry about cavities or the other evils of sweet treats. That is not to say that our children don't like candy—they do! But many also like the tasty and nutritious treats that their mothers and fathers, and grandmothers and grandfathers, ate when they were small.

Early Hopis, hard at work in the fields or otherwise engaged in getting food for the family, didn't have the time or inclination to eat between meals. Nor did the earlier Indians eat many sweet foods, although some did chew on cornmeal to extract the corn sugars. A few fruits, such as melons, peaches, apricots, apples, and grapes, that grow readily in the good soil below the mesas or can be purchased from peddlars or fruit markets, have become popular, however, especially among the children. The fruit is eaten fresh or, frequently, is dried and stored for later use. Various seeds, such as pumpkin and squash seeds, or green cottonwood seeds, are also popular, and so are cattail pods. Parched corn is a very old Indian recipe that is eaten both as a snack and in main dishes.

Popcorn is a specific species of corn and is probably consumed more by Anglos than Indians.

PUMPKIN SEEDS (Patngo Vosee)

1. Soak seeds in salt water (1 tablespoon salt dissolved in 1 cup of water) for a half hour or longer.
2. Drain seeds and spread in a shallow pan.
3. Roast in a 350°F oven for fifteen to twenty minutes, or until lightly browned.
4. Cushaw seeds are best.

Squash and sunflower seeds can also be roasted in this way. These seeds are good as a snack, or, when dropped into the center of rolled piki, as a sandwich.

PIÑON NUTS (Tuva)

1. Clean and sort nuts, removing any foreign matter or unsavory nuts.
2. Wash nuts in clear water, two or three times, to remove dirt.
3. Put nuts in a pan and roast in a 350°F oven for about twenty minutes, stirring every five minutes to prevent them from burning. Crack open a shell to check for doneness. When ready, nuts will be light brown in color.
4. Make a salt brine by dissolving 1 tablespoon salt in 1 cup of water. Sprinkle brine lightly on the nuts, stirring well, and return nuts to the oven to dry. (A salt shaker is good for sprinkling brine.)
5. Cool nuts before serving.

Roasted piñons, with an added touch of salt, are a real taste treat. They are usually served to friends who drop in after supper and are considered a luxury. The nuts are gathered in the fall, when they drop from the pine cones of the various piñon trees, and are usually reserved for visiting friends and relatives. In the past, when the harvest work was completed, clan history and prophesies were often shared by the grandmother around a bowl of freshly roasted piñons.

PARCHED CORN (Kutuki)

1. Heat clean, fine sand in a cast iron pot until it becomes dark brown and hot (water sprinkled on it should sizzle and pop).
2. Pour in a cup or two of dried corn. (Old corn will be crunchy; this year's corn will be harder.)
3. Stir corn briskly, to keep it from burning, until it stops popping.
4. Remove corn from sand with a sieve and pour into a bowl.
5. Sprinkle corn with salt water (1 tablespoon salt dissolved in 1 cup of water), and stir with a corn cob that has been dipped in the salt water.
6. Add piñons or peach pits for variety.

The reservation has very sandy soil, so sand of the right quality for parching corn and beans is readily available. Furthermore, it doesn't cling like the moist sands of coastal areas but readily falls away from the toasted foods. Any color corn can be parched and makes a delicious and nutritious snack.

PARCHED BEANS

1. Heat clean, fine sand in a cast iron pot until it becomes dark brown and hot. Test sand by dropping in a bean; if it browns quickly, the sand is hot enough. Or drop a little water on the sand; if it sputters, the sand is hot.
2. Wash and sort several cups of white tepary beans or other small, white beans. Older beans from last year work best.
3. Pour beans into sand and stir briskly to keep them from burning.
4. When beans have browned lightly, remove them from the sand with a sieve and pour them into a bowl.
5. Sprinkle beans with salt water (1 tablespoon salt dissolved in 1 cup of water), and stir well.

This recipe comes from the western part of the reservation and was often served by my husband's grandmother and cousins, especially at Christmastime. I am told that parched beans are often the first salty food to be served to Hopis who are ending a fast.

DRYING PEACHES AND OTHER FRUIT

1. Wash fruit thoroughly and either split in half or cut into slices.
2. Spread fruit on a drying rack or other suitable surface and put in the sun to dry.
3. Cover fruit with cheesecloth or nylon netting, to keep out flies and dust. Protect the fruit also from rain.
4. Turn fruit daily to ensure even drying. Fruit will take several days to dry completely.
5. Store fruit in covered containers in cool, dry place.

When I first came to Hopi country, the women of Hotevilla formed "work parties" when the peaches were ripe, to sweep the dirt off the rocks at the edge of the village, split the newly harvested fruit, and lay it on the hot rocks to dry. This was a community project and many of the women joined in. Other villages also formed such work parties, but Hotevilla is the fruit-growing center of the reservation and, consequently, had many peaches to be picked and stored. Unfortunately, weather patterns began changing in northern Arizona in the late sixties, and we haven't had a good fruit crop in recent years because of late freezes. So, the pleasurable and productive get-togethers have become unnecessary and have gradually been discontinued.

DRIED MUSKMELON

1. Peel very ripe muskmelons or cantalopes, cut in half, and remove seeds.
2. Slice flesh in thin, continuous spiral strips, going round and round the melons.
3. Cover fruit with cheesecloth or nylon netting, to protect it from flies, dust, and rain. (Nylon netting makes a particularly good cover as it doesn't stick to the fruit and keeps out even small insects.)
4. Put fruit in the sun to dry. Turn strips daily to ensure even drying. (It will take several days for the fruit to dry completely.)

Muskmelon is a favorite of our children, and apparently also of our cats. One day I spread some melon strips on my drying rack, covered them with nylon netting, and left them on my screened-in porch to dry. The next day, when I went out to turn the strips, they were gone—my cats had had a feast. When I mentioned this to other homemakers, I found that they, too, had trouble keeping cats out of their melon.

Special
Information

Hopi Foods for Fasting

In the Hopi religion there are times when abstinence from certain foods is required. Hopis believe that the self denial practiced during a fast brings about a closer relationship with the Creator. Fasting both purifies the body and makes the will stronger.

Hopis usually fast for four days before any sacred ceremonial. During this time they abstain completely from salt and any food containing fat, such as meat, nuts, and dairy products.

Listed below are samples of the foods a modern Hopi may eat during a religious fast.

Prepare all dishes without salt or fat

Beans
Blue marbles
Cream of wheat
Fruits (fresh, dried, or canned), such as
    apples, peaches, melons, or raisins
Greens
Oatmeal
Piki
Pumpkin, baked
Rice, boiled, with sugar
Salads (vegetable or fruit), no dressing
Someviki (blue, white, or whole wheat)
Squash, baked
Sweet corn mush
Tomatoes
Tortillas (blue or white)

Beverages

Coffee
Kool-aid
Tea
Sepal Tocie

Mineral Content of Selected Hopi Foods

Sample Identification	Grams per Kilogram						
	Solids	N	Na	K	Ca	Mg	P
Blue cornmeal	924	17.02	0.04	4.14	0.09	1.40	3.72
Pink cornmeal	904	18.04	0.10	3.80	0.06	1.39	3.98
Dry white corn	920	15.66	0.01	3.57	0.08	1.40	3.89
White cornmeal	914	17.20	0.02	3.61	0.11	1.36	3.83
Dried roasted sweet corn, boiled	961	25.74	0.06	5.99	0.34	1.48	3.97
Piki bread	905	16.73	1.06	7.00	1.40	1.90	3.36
Hominy	925	18.72	0.04	7.86	0.16	1.76	3.67
Bigami (corn and sprouted wheat)	916	16.37	0.07	3.55	0.27	1.25	2.99

Sample Identification	Milligrams per Kilogram									
	Mn	Fe	Ni	Cu	Zn	Se	Br	Rb	Sr	Pb
Blue cornmeal	7±1	32±1	1.3±.4	3.0±.4	26±1	<0.9	5.1±.4	<1.7	<2.1	1.4±.5
Pink cornmeal	9±1	34±1	1.1±.5	2.9±.5	33±1	<1.2	1.1±.5	<2.2	<2.7	13±1
White cornmeal	9±1	30±1	1.1±.4	3.1±.4	31±1	<0.9	4.3±.4	1.1±.5	<2.0	<1.6
Dried roasted sweet corn, boiled	23±1	71±3	3.6±.4	20±1	75±3	2.3±.3	2.7±.4	1.3±.6	3.2±.8	4.6±.6
Piki bread	14±1	84±4	1.0±.4	4.5±.4	36±2	<0.8	12±1	4.3±.5	13±1	2±1
Hominy	8±1	27±1	1.2±.4	2.7±.7	37±1	<0.9	1.1±.4	2.1±.6	2.7±.7	<1.6
Bigami (corn and sprouted wheat)	13±1	35±2	0.6±.3	3.3±.3	32±2	<0.7	<9.1	1.8±.4	3.4±.5	4±1

Source: Adapted by the author from D. H. Calloway, R. D. Giauque, and F. M. Costa, "The Superior Mineral Content of Some American Indian Foods in Comparison to Federally Donated Counterpart Commodities," *Ecology of Food and Nutrition* 3 (July 1974):205.

Index